Tansy's Tales
By
Jennifer Rae

Copyright Notices

Published under the Copyright Laws of the Library of Congress of the United States of America by:

Jennifer Rae Trojan Publishing
West Chicago, Illinois
kessenskronikles@gmail.com

International Standard Book Number
(ISBN) 978-0-9978633-0-7

Cover Photos
Wall of Fame Photo
©2016 by Kim Stephenson – PawPrints Pix Photography

Cover Design
2016 by Pam Osbourne

Disclaimer

This is a work of fiction. Names, characters, places, events and incidents are either the products of the author's imagination or used in a fictitious manner.

Because the dog is the storyteller, the rules regarding proper grammar and punctuation are loosely followed.

Books by Jennifer Rae:
Kessen's Kronikles
The Adventures of a Cross Country Canine
and
Izzy Come…Izzy Go

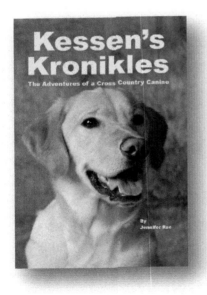
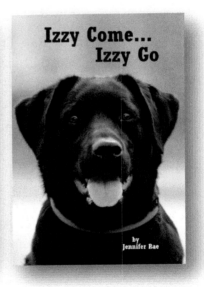

DEDICATION

To Kessen

He meant so much to so many.

TABLE OF CONTENTS

INTRODUCTION

Two mischievous dogs...an energetic, black Labrador Retriever and the other an audacious, blonde mix of Labrador Retriever and Golden Retriever...suddenly find themselves unsupervised in the house while their folks rush the family's other dog to the animal hospital. Will these two dogs run amuck with their surprising freedom, or are they bound by training and pack rules to behave reasonably under these conditions? While the prospect of impish behavior is more than just appealing, mature and responsible dogs most often choose wisely. Do these two playful dogs fit this description, or will they run rampant through the house with this unintentional gift of freedom?

As the main character and storyteller, I can only say that what happens on this particular day is based upon accurate occurrences...that is, of course, as I participated in them, witnessed them or was told about them by our pack leader. Am I biased in terms of my descriptions of what transpires during the day? Perhaps to some degree, I am. Does the possibility of bias make the events any less truthful in terms of the contents of my stories? Most assuredly, it does not. If nothing else, I rely entirely upon my integrity for accurate reporting of events because that's my primary responsibility as the storyteller.

This is a day that will long be remembered not only by me, the storyteller, but also by all of the members of the household…and perhaps even by you, the reader. So, please join me as I share the memories told to me by my beloved pack leader as well as those I experienced during my journey. By sharing them with you, the reader, they become and will always remain…Tansy's Tales.

Shall we begin?

PART I
MORNING

The sorority house, appropriately named for all the female canines who have crossed the threshold over the years, is considerably quiet today. Our foster folks, lovingly called mom and dad, left earlier this morning in a great hurry with Kessen, our pack leader. He wasn't feeling too well, and I'm guessing that they took him to the animal hospital. I'm not sure what to think about the situation, but I'm hoping that everything will be okay for Kessen. I really trust the doctors at the animal hospital, so I know that he is in good hands.

The Storyteller

My name is Tansy, and I'm third in command of all things canine when the folks are out of the house. In the world of human politics, I'd be the Speaker of the House and not likely to ever be in charge. The chain of command is actually the same in the canine world. I'm a black, energetic Labrador Retriever whose position in the pack order is not assigned because of some substandard behavior on my part. You see, I was away from the pack for many years while working as an assistance dog to a wonderful person. Upon my retirement from service, I was welcomed back to my foster parents' home as well as to the canine pack. This fact alone surprised me because I was a bit of a paw-full in my youth as a puppy in training. Coming back to the household after so many years determined my position in the pack. Kessen is and always will be the pack leader…no question about that. The way I look at it, he is in charge, and I'm his *facilitator extraordinaire*. Do you recognize a sense of self-importance in that description of myself? I do tend to think rather highly of myself and, regrettably, am often the only one who does.

Our folks have been puppy raisers for potential assistance dogs for the past fourteen years. They get a puppy when he or she is only eight weeks old and are responsible for the puppy's socialization, basic obedience, proper leash behavior and public etiquette. They have twelve to fifteen months to accomplish these goals. All of us at the sorority house went through this training when we were puppies. For me, it was a day-to-day roller coaster ride full of adventures and excitement. Those days were so memorable!

Returning to the sorority house a few months ago was like coming full circle in my life, and I'm taking every opportunity to enjoy my return to the fullest. Kessen leaving so quickly to go the animal hospital puts a damper on my enjoyment, but I'm hoping the folks have everything under control in terms of his care. While feelings of apprehension are swirling through my mind, I'm keeping my paws crossed for Kessen's well-being.

These same troublesome feelings are shared with my best friend and confidante named Brightie. She is another

member of the pack and has quite an innocent look about her. However, don't be fooled by the sincere kindness depicted in those expressive, chocolate-colored eyes and curly eyelashes. Even though we tend to get caught by the folks each time we try something naughty, she enjoys mischief just as much as I do.

The Best Friend

Another mischief maker and honorary member of our pack is an energetic, black Labrador Retriever named Harley. Because he spends occasional weekends at our house, we call him our Weekend Warrior. He's just the cutest puppy, but his teeth double as sharpened pins. Unfortunately, we are his own personal pin cushions. Kessen, as pack leader, usually keeps the little tyke in line. Harley, in turn, fully accepts his mentoring. Even at such an early age, Harley knows better than to

The Weekend Warrior

go against the leader of the pack's guidance. Brightie and I, as minions in the pack, are just collateral damage in terms of Harley's learning curve and his use of those hazardous teeth. While this is a terrible thought to admit, both of us yearn for the day that Harley loses those dangerous weapons disguised as puppy teeth.

It's fortunate that Harley is spending this weekend at his foster family's house. If he had been here and the folks mistakenly left him loose in their hurried trip to the animal hospital with Kessen, the house would be a total mess by the time they came home. Harley, being so young, has no boundaries in terms of self-control. That little rascal shreds whatever is within his grasp and eats anything he comes across on the floor. Fortunately, Harley is well supervised and enjoying quality kennel-time at his other place of residence. At the same time, our house is safe from total destruction.

Without Harley's endless playfulness, Brightie and I can concentrate of what is going on here at the house. Whatever is happening with Kessen can't be very good. We know this to be true because the folks left with him in such a hurry, and they never leave the house without going through a certain ritual. Their routine begins by turning the television on in the sunroom. By doing that, we are supposed to believe that they are still somewhere in the house. We humor them by going along with their ruse even though we know full well that they're preparing to go out. Just before they leave, they have us go into our kennels located in the sunroom. We don't mind kennel time since our kennels guarantee safety and comfort when the folks aren't at home. Furthermore, if left unsupervised, we tend to get into all sorts of trouble. Let's be honest…that's really the main reason for kenneling us.

Our mom says that we have impulse-control issues when left alone and free to roam the house. Just because the folks left us unsupervised on one occasion and came home to a shredded dog bed doesn't mean that we don't deserve a second chance. Of course, our having tufts of bed-stuffing hanging from our mouths didn't help our cause either. In our defense, it was an old bed that wasn't able to withstand the rigors of a good game of Tug of War. Since we were always expected to pick up our toys, playthings were never left lying around. What other options did we have? That old bed was just an unintended casualty in our game to amuse ourselves in her absence. Out of necessity, we were forced to improvise in the selection of appropriate toys.

Of course, Kessen wasn't included in our disciplinary consequences. According to the folks, he wouldn't dream of doing such a thing…another perk of being leader of the pack. Because Brightie and I don't speak Human, we were unable to give our side of the story, and Kessen remained the innocent, safe bystander. If our mother would have checked the inside of his mouth, she would have found a mass of bed-stuffing hidden behind his

He looked so innocent.

sparkling white teeth. Instead, Kessen just looked up at her with those huge brown eyes that literally screamed of innocence. She didn't even see his mischievous wink while we were sternly lectured about the importance of keeping our mouths off all things not approved as appropriate toys. Kessen always got away with things…apparently, his distinction as pack leader commanded total respect and complete absolution from any wrongdoings. That being said, he still enjoyed occasional mischief knowing full well that he'd not be held

11

accountable for any damage in the process. It certainly was great to be the king!

Getting back to the events of today, this newly-found freedom serves as a menu for mischief and mayhem. I'd like to blame Brightie and say that she is, indeed, the instigator of all things naughty, but that wouldn't be fair or accurate. I, too, enjoy a bit of mischief now and then but rarely get the chance to act on that enjoyment. When the folks are ready to go out somewhere, they give us our command words to go into our kennels. Kessen's kennel command is Holiday Inn, and Brightie's is Red Roof Inn. While their commands seem quite creative, Harley and I aren't so lucky in the command department and are simply given the word Kennel as our command. How uninspired is that? Somehow I think we got short changed with that totally unimaginative and ordinary command. While it certainly lacks the pizazz and creativity of Kessen's and Brightie's commands, perhaps the lack of ingenuity is meant to remind us of our pack positions. Still, a bit of flair with the command word would have been appreciated. Nevertheless, upon hearing those words, we march like obedient soldiers into our appointed kennels, assume sitting positions and get treats before the kennel doors are closed. It isn't such a bad gig since we get to think about the day's events, enjoy uninterrupted sleep and perhaps dream of great escapades. Being kenneled is really quite a relaxing time for us, and who doesn't like having their very own room? I'll never understand why some dogs howl and bark when placed in their kennels…it's such a pleasant place to rest. I try to make the most of my kennel time and enjoy the peace and quiet. It energizes me for the next adventures.

However, this morning we are left entirely on our own. If we suddenly get the urge to run around the house at full speed, fling chew toys around the room or shred toilet paper from the ring in the bathroom, we have free rein to do whatever we choose. After all, these mischievous acts are all possible since there is no one here to stop us. If we really want to assert our friskiness, we might even

Let's have some fun!

jump on the couch. I know that doesn't sound like the height of mischief, but being on furniture is a real No-No in our world. Furniture hopping is considered one of the most serious infractions in our household...except, of course, for Kessen. He can do anything he wants to do as yet another advantage of being the pack leader. That dog certainly has it made!

So Brightie and I wander around the house knowing that there are numerous opportunities for fun and adventure. Should we have a game of toss with a decorative throw pillow from the couch? After all, just the words *throw pillow* imply as well as encourage that sort of game. Yanking threads from some of the numerous rugs that form a path covering the slippery, ceramic tile is also entertaining. While these rugs do save us from sliding when we forget that running isn't allowed in the house, the occasional loose threads are just begging for some energetic tugs. Brightie and I might just make a game of who can pull the most threads in a short period of time. What about scooping up some of the dirt from the planter in the living room...the one that holds the tall, artificial Ficus tree? If we do, we could scatter heaps of dirt all over the sun room floor. Howls of "Dirt Fight...Dirt Fight" always get the adrenalin going even though it creates a mess...not to mention the dirt that covers our mouths after the fun subsides. On the other paw, nothing is ever totally wonderful since mischievous acts are usually followed by consequences. However, penalties usually occur after the fun which makes being caught worth the risk.

As we saunter through the house, nothing seems to grab our attention in terms of mischief. After thinking about it, we both come up with the reason: it's never fun when the element of risk is missing. Kessen isn't here to purse his lips and give us the *stink-eye* denoting disappointment in our behavior, and the folks aren't even here to make the risk worthwhile. Let's face it...being caught in the act is half the fun of getting into trouble.

With that thought in mind, Brightie and I decide that mischief just isn't as interesting when there is no threat involved. We slowly walk the path on the rugs covering the slippery floor tiles, pass the decorative pillows on the couch, glance at the Ficus tree that's safe in its dirt-filled planter and find our way to the sun room where our kennels await us. As if hearing our commands, we both enter our kennels, assume sitting positions and just gaze at the open kennel doors. The only things missing in this process are the treats!

While my kennel is sparse and has only wires for walls, Brightie's is a bit more decorative. On the wall at the far end of her kennel hangs a first place, blue ribbon. It's one of her cherished possessions…even better than a dog bone filled with peanut butter. Its placement on a certain wall is also significant because Brightie thoroughly believes in the merits of *feng shui* as a means of attaining tranquility in her life. Having that precious ribbon on her specific kennel wall is essential. Even though I am occasionally a bit critical of her beliefs, I think this belief has its merits.

The ribbon on Brightie's kennel wall was won by a dog named Izzy. She spent her training days at the sorority house and won that ribbon for amazing work in agility. Izzy dreamt of eventually becoming a champion athlete…complete with ribbons and trophies. Brightie, being Izzy's soul mate, lived vicariously through those dreams. Even though Izzy reached her goal in agility, she chose instead to go into the world of assistance to others. When Izzy was ready to go off to advanced

training, she surprised Brightie by leaving her blue ribbon as a gift for her. Knowing Brightie's total reliance on *feng shui* for serenity in her life, the blue ribbon was placed on the appropriate kennel wall as a tribute to their friendship. Each time Brightie enters her kennel, she's reminded of Izzy and their shared bond…a

Izzy's Special Gift

comforting bond of friendship that will last forever. That's *feng shui* at its best.

Having been momentarily mesmerized by the blue ribbon in Brightie's kennel, I suddenly realize that each of us chose to enter our kennels rather than run rampant through the house. We are doing the responsible thing, and how disappointing is that for two energetic dogs left to their own devices in an unsupervised household? The decision to forfeit an opportunity for mischief in lieu of responsible behavior is puzzling, but apparently, waiting for Kessen's return in the comfort of our kennels is the right thing to do. Brightie is already fast asleep in her kennel by the time I realize that we are possibly showing signs of maturity. Did I feel relief or disappointment over the possibility? Rather than waste my mental energy on that issue, I choose to just relax and take in the serenity of the quiet household.

Looking around the sun room, I happen to glance at the wall opposite our kennels. Our folks affectionately refer to it as the Wall of Fame because it holds pictures of all of the dogs

The Wall of Fame

who have spent time in the sorority house while training for assistance. Surrounded by frames of various colors, textures and sizes, so many faces stare back at me in expressive poses. They remind me of how lucky I am to not only have a space on the wall but to be a part of such a special family.

Since I returned to the sorority house a few months ago, Kessen has been telling me all sorts of stories about the dogs who have been a part of his life here and not just the dogs who have merited space on the walls. He has so many stories to tell about the dogs who have made an impact on the household residents. I find that I'm like a lint-removing sponge that attempts to absorb every detail of the adventures he shares.

Kessen's stories are the best!

When I was just a young and feisty puppy, I spent a lively weekend at the sorority house. Years later, I was reminded that constantly tormenting Kessen, Brightie and a dog-in-training named Izzy was my weekend form of amusement. While I remembered the weekend quite differently, I didn't dare disagree with Kessen's version out of respect for his leadership position and keeper of the memories.

After that memorable weekend, I visited another family for a while, but then returned to the sorority house to complete my puppy training. Months later after spending quality time with Kessen, Brightie and Izzy, I moved on to advanced training followed by a career in assistance. Since I was gone from the sorority house for quite a while, Kessen has been filling me in on all that has happened. I really missed a lot of household and neighborhood activities by being in service, but I now welcome every one of Kessen's stories.

You see, Kessen is the respected neighborhood storyteller and known for his incredible ability to make a story come alive through his words. Dogs from all over the neighborhood gather on the back deck for his storytelling time, and Kessen's stories never disappoint them. The fact that Kessen is willing to share these missed adventures and stories with me is truly an honor. I can't wait until he comes back home with the folks so we can continue our storytelling time.

Kessen is quite a storyteller!

Listening to Brightie snoring away next door to my kennel makes me momentarily wish I had more than wires for kennel walls. That canine snores like a farm animal! On the other paw, her snoring has somewhat of a soothing cadence that is lulling me into a sense of calmness that has been missing during these past hours. While waiting for news about Kessen's health, I find myself gazing at the Wall of Fame and thinking about each of these special dogs. Perhaps if I relive their individual tales as told to me by Kessen, it just might help pass the time until the folks return with him.

So, whose tale will be the first to occupy my mind and share with you, the reader? Scanning the faces framed in various poses staring back at me from the Wall of Fame, I should begin with the most important one…Kessen, the pack leader. However, I believe that I will stray from the usual protocol and pack-behavior expectations. Instead, I choose to begin with the story of the very first puppy who came to the sorority house a few years before Kessen even arrived. Sammy, the Golden Retriever who lives next door, first told this story to Kessen who passed it on to me so that I might continue his legacy as storyteller. This story is the first of many adventures that will be shared today and is the beginning of what I refer to as Tansy's Tales…

Sammy tells all!

PART II
AFTERNOON
Tales from The Wall of Fame

Turin

The afternoon sun is now shining brightly through the sunroom windows, and I am ready to begin my first attempt at storytelling. Gazing at the Wall of Fame, my eyes focused on the photo of Turin...the fair-haired, male Labrador Retriever who was the first of many puppies to enter the sorority house as an assistance dog in training. Of course, the house wasn't called the sorority house yet. That name would come later when female dogs seemed to take over the pack order. But, it was the beginning of an adventure for Turin...far beyond his puppy expectations.

He came from sunny California and traveled via his first and only airplane ride to the Midwest with his sister. It was an uneventful flight, but Turin knew that when the plane landed, he would meet his new puppy raiser family. That thought was both thrilling and anxiety producing. What if this new family didn't like him? Was he too small or too thin? So many questions remained unanswered until the plane landed.

Concerned Puppy

His sister, who was his traveling companion, shared the same thoughts and concerns. Their other brothers and sisters, who stayed in California, told far-fetched stories of the many evils of going to a new home. Perhaps, they were just trying to get them all riled up about a new place that would change their lives. Maybe they were even somewhat jealous since they weren't going for an airplane ride and most likely never would. These thoughts definitely helped to lessen feelings of anxiety.

When the airplane landed, the excitement and apprehension returned in the form of shrill howling and loud barking. From the pups' point of view, they were just saying a nervous and loud *hello* to their new families. Personally, I don't think that the new families interpreted the harshness of sounds coming from the airline crate in the same manner. Since I wasn't there, I'll just stick to the story as it was told to me.

When their airline crate was opened, the puppies saw smiling faces looking back at them. These people didn't even know them, yet they already seemed to like them. All of the pups' worries during the flight were in vain as each individual gave them hugs and kisses. Turin and his sister were having such a good time and hoped that their time together would never end, but that was just wishful thinking on their part. They were going to different families, and soon it was time for them to say goodbye to each other. Turin hoped that he might see his sister again someday, but even if they didn't meet in the future, they still shared a bond…the bond of family that would stay with them forever.

Turin was now in his very first home and seemed to readily adapt to this new and thrilling life. He had been named by the service organization when he was born, but he really didn't know what name they had given him. He supposed that he'd eventually find this out once he got settled in his new place. Sure enough, his training as a potential assistance dog began immediately, and the focus was on his responding to his new given-name of Turin and doing something called a Sit. He really liked the name assigned to him but didn't see the sense of doing that Sit stuff. Everything was so much easier to do when standing on all four paws, but he went along with the training program because he enjoyed getting the treats

Turin began his training.

when successful. Little did he know that those treats were really parts of his breakfast, lunch and dinner put aside for training purposes. The pup didn't know that he was shortchanged at meals early in his life, but it was done to keep him healthy and maintain appropriate weight. Since he could eat all day long without taking a breath, it was probably in his best interest to follow this routine.

A significant experience for Turin was his first play date. While he wasn't sure just what a play date was, anything that involved a car ride was, by nature, an exciting event. Once safely secured in the car's portable crate, Turin and our mom were off to their new adventure. Turin's head moved from side to side as he tried to take in all of the highway sights on the way to their destination. Finally, they arrived at a beautiful house with a huge circular driveway. Our mom carefully carried him out of his crate and placed him on the stone driveway that looked like little pebbles stuck together. It was a very colorful driveway, and since the sun was shining, those pebbles seemed to sparkle. Standing on them made the pads of his paws tingle, but the weird feeling was quickly forgotten as they enthusiastically made their way from the car and up the driveway to the house.

Turin thoroughly enjoyed meeting new people but certainly wasn't expecting what was about to happen. When that door opened, he was greeted by our mom's friend and two enthusiastic canines. One of the dogs was an older, rather large, yellow Labrador Retriever named Jake, and the other was a tiny, snow-white West Highland Terrier called Tyke. Because Tyke was so small, Turin couldn't quite figure out his age, but that didn't matter because they seemed quite happy to see him. Engaging in the proper canine etiquette for greetings, they sniffed each other's body parts…starting at the rear. While that seems an unusual and possibly gross practice to humans, it is totally acceptable in the canine community. In fact, it is an essential aspect of proper canine etiquette.

Once this formality was completed, all three dogs rushed through the house, ran down the stairs and went off to play in the yard. Jake and Tyke were mismatched due to their sizes, but the discrepancy didn't alter their speed and ability to maneuver through the bushes in the yard. Although much larger in stature, Jake was careful not to bump or push Turin in any way as the energetic puppy followed their lead through the greenery. Tyke, on the other paw, was a rough and tough player, so Turin was careful to avoid running into him. The pooches ran, played, barked and howled with glee until exhaustion set in, and sleep took over. Before he lapsed into dreamland, Turin hoped that he'd get another chance to play with Jake and Tyke later in the day.

However, the excitement and fun experienced during play time turned to concern when Turin woke up and went to the water bowl for a drink. Unlike most puppies with their pudgy bodies, Turin was quite thin and depending upon the way he stood, his ribs were showing just a bit through his fair-haired coat. When our mom and her friend looked down at him as he drank, they spotted a single rib protruding quite a bit from under his coat. They couldn't recall it looking like that before he played. Concern over Turin's well-being took precedence over the enthusiasm of the play date. While Turin didn't seem affected by the position of his rib, our mom wasn't quite sure what to do. As Turin drank the water, that rib seemed to move in unison with his drinking. While it looked a bit bizarre, it didn't seem to bother Turin.

Nevertheless, our mom felt differently about the rib situation. Since she'd pass the animal hospital on the way home, she'd have Turin's rib checked by the veterinarian. Feelings of guilt filled her mind as she neared the animal hospital. If it turned out that he had hurt himself while playing so enthusiastically with the other dogs, perhaps the play date wasn't such a good idea. Cradling Turin's tiny, fifteen-pound body in her arms, she gently took him from the car into the animal hospital and waited for the doctor in the exam room.

Within a few minutes, the kind doctor, who gave Turin his first examination a few weeks earlier, came into the room and had our mom place Turin on the exam table. After careful examination of Turin's ribs, the doctor indicated that Turin had something called a *floating rib*. Apparently, it wasn't anything unusual since growing puppies still had to develop strength in their bones and muscles. During this growth period, sometimes the *floating rib* would be visible. It was nothing to be concerned about and would eventually disappear as the puppy grew older and developed strength in his muscles.

While our mom was relieved at the news, her earlier feelings of guilt now changed to those of foolishness over her haste in taking Turin to the animal hospital. Although it might have been the first time she felt this way, it certainly wasn't going to be the last. Turin's well-being was a definite priority, and from her point of view, it was better to be safe than sorry. Little did she know that a number of trips to the animal hospital with Turin were in her future. This tiny puppy would not just grow in size and strength in the months to come. He would develop a talent for daredevil tactics that both amazed and frightened everyone in the household. She had a frequent flyer on her hands and didn't even know it.

Turin gradually learned a few other commands and quickly advanced to wearing his service cape and special collar...sometimes called a head collar. Since he couldn't go out in public places until fully vaccinated, Turin practiced wearing his service gear for short periods of time while at home. Although every day was an adventure for him, his world revolved around his house, the huge yard and the driveway.

When he was about four months old, he was fully vaccinated and ready for adventures in public. Now, our mom and dad took him on longer walks as well as visits to neighboring parks. Since he wore his head collar, some people thought he was wearing a muzzle and even asked if he wore it because he had a tendency to bite. That made Turin chuckle because it wasn't a muzzle at all, and the thought of biting someone never crossed his mind. Actual biting was never

He was dressed for the job.

ever an acceptable act...especially during his public training sessions. Turin would never intentionally do anything unacceptable in public because he took great pride in his behavior while wearing his training gear. People were inclined to ask about him and his training when they saw him approach. The spotlight was entirely on him and his behavior, and he thoroughly enjoyed every minute of it.

His new family showered him with countless praise when his behavior was appropriate, but they never really drew undue attention to the things that he did incorrectly. That inconsistency confused him a bit, but he heard that it had to do with something called positive reinforcement...rewarding good behavior and ignoring the bad stuff. While Turin really didn't know what positive reinforcement was, as long as he wasn't getting punished for some of his questionable actions, he thought it was a great philosophy of life.

On the other paw, he realized that there was a down side to positive reinforcement. Because the folks were new at puppy raising, they were a bit over-protective at times and often responsible for what was referred to as *handler error* in the canine community. That occurred when the dog did something incorrectly because the handler unintentionally directed him to do it. One of the most common examples of *handler error* in Turin's experiences was the accidental combination of two

separate commands. Sit and Down were given as one command: Sit/Down. Did our mom want him to Sit or to assume the Down position? It was confusing to Turin who wanted to please our mom by doing it correctly, but he didn't know how to do both at the

This idea sounded interesting.

same time. On the plus side, incidents of *handler error* were considered *get-out-of-jail* free cards in Turin's mind, and the possibilities for doing all types of creative behaviors were limitless.

According to Turin, his good or bad actions were teaching tools that helped his family adjust to their new role as puppy raisers. He considered this approach to teaching as his duty to all puppy raisers as well as service to the canine community. He learned what behaviors might not be acceptable without being given a penalty, and the folks learned from their unintentional mistakes. It was the perfect living and training experience for both...or so he thought.

I have to admit, Turin was one shrewd pup and had a great game going on with that line of thought. Nevertheless, I needed to stick to the story as Sammy told it to Kessen and not offer my opinions. I assumed this was the job of a good storyteller, and I intended to be the best...or at least the next best following Kessen's mentoring.

Turin was becoming an exceptional puppy, and it wasn't long before his athletic talents and death-defying actions were duly noted by his foster family. These types of behaviors did not fall within the category of *handler error*. Turin's name was written all over them as individual attempts toward stardom. He maintained the record as the first and only dog who launched himself at full speed over the back of the couch in the living room. This daredevil stunt won him the distinctive nickname of T-Man. What's even more exceptional was that he was only four months old at the time. To this day, no dog has ever attempted such a feat of athletic prowess in the sorority house. Not only was launching himself into the air becoming a daily activity for him, this reckless behavior was becoming a great concern for his foster family as well.

Some of his attempts at being a frequent flyer didn't end so positively in terms of becoming record breaking. During one of his full-flight antics, he snagged his teeth on a strap from his mother's purse...while she was holding it. The result of this launch was the loss of sections from two of his four-month old baby teeth. If he had yanked them out entirely, it wouldn't have been so detrimental, but the possibility of infection due to portions of his splintered teeth being exposed was a most

This flight didn't end well.

definite concern. So, a critical decision was made, and it was unquestionably way beyond Turin's expectations.

He was originally scheduled to be neutered at the age of six months, but since parts of those two teeth were partially exposed, the veterinarian would pack the exposed teeth to avoid infection and neuter him at the same time. Turin was in for what they called a very special *two-fer* resulting from his faulty launch. Since Turin didn't even know what neutering was, he wasn't at all apprehensive about the entire experience. In his four-month old puppy mind, he was a free spirit, and this so-called neutering was just another new experience.

Following his recuperation from the purse-launch consequence, Turin continued with his daredevil antics in his free time. The neutering that resulted from his purse-launch didn't bother him at all. He was older now and definitely more powerful in terms of his jumping abilities. As a pup in training for possible assistance, his days were filled with attending obedience classes, learning numerous commands and preparing for public outings. His foster folks were getting more adept at avoiding *handler error*, so he was now being held accountable for most of his actions.

Sloppy Sits were comfortable.

Truth be told, he enjoyed learning his commands and just loved the praise the folks would offer when he did something well. They truly believed in using positive reinforcement as a training tool. Whenever Turin would practice his Sit command nicely without being told, he'd be rewarded with lavish praise. It worked with other commands as well, but he believed his Sits were the best. Unfortunately, some Sits were considered a bit sloppy with his legs comfortably positioned out to the side, but he didn't care. That position made him look a bit like a tripod gone off-center, but comfort was a priority at this time of his life. Nevertheless, he enjoyed their praise whenever he got it and looked for opportunities to be rewarded.

On one particular day, Turin was running around the house looking for some form of mischief when he spotted the ideal place to demonstrate his perfect use of the Sit command. The folks called it a coffee table, but to Turin, it was an elevated platform that would highlight his perfect Sit. It wasn't as high as the other tables in the house, but it was the perfect place to demonstrate his ability to Sit properly. He was ecstatic over the possibility of the praise that would follow with this accomplishment.

Planning was a necessity for success in terms of this new challenge. Walking around the coffee table numerous times and checking all surrounding areas, Turin realized that while a narrow wooden frame bordered the table, the clear surface in the center might be slippery. He would have to practice this launch before the folks witnessed his newest endeavor. In preparation for the challenge, he circled the room a few times, gathered some speed and jumped onto the platform. He knew immediately that his speed was too great since he quickly lost his balance on the center's clear surface, slid off the platform and bounced into the front of the couch. He hadn't anticipated just how slippery the surface was nor did he measure his speed accurately. He'd definitely have to adjust his speed...by a lot!

After circling the platform a few more times, he took a running start at a slower speed and was able to jump, skid to a stop in the middle of the slippery surface and lower his body

Jennifer Rae

into a perfect sitting position. Filled with pride over his accomplishment, he was now ready to demonstrate his new skill to the folks.

After a quick dismount from the platform, Turin searched the house for his intended audience. Hearing the folks in the hall, he got their attention by running around the room at great speed while narrowly missing the edges of the platform as he ran by. He knew that they'd follow him because running wasn't allowed in the house. Seeing Turin so close to the edges of the table alerted the folks to what he might just be attempting to do. Color drained from their faces as they realized that Turin was going to launch all thirty pounds of Labrador Retriever onto the glass top of their coffee table. Would the glass shatter under Turin's weight? Would he be terribly hurt by the broken glass? Panic was about to overtake them when they realized it was too late to stop Turin's launch. As if the event occurred in slow motion, they held their breath as they watched him fly through the air. The folks could only hope for the best outcome when Turin landed.

Turin landed safely in the middle of the glass coffee table, turned to them and ended in a perfect sitting position. Pride filled his face as he waited for their lavish praise. Instead, his audience was totally silent. The folks' ashen faces reflected both fear and relief that up until this point, the glass was still intact. They didn't want to startle him due to the potential for his falling through the center of the table if the glass broke under his weight, so they slowly advanced toward their thirty-pound bundle of daredevil puppy.

When they reached him, they praised his perfect Sit, but then quickly gave him the Off command to leave the surface. While disappointed over not even being given time to enjoy his praise, he reluctantly left his position on the platform which the folks referred to as a glass coffee table. He didn't know what glass was, and why they were so frightened by his accomplishment? Every now and then, he felt that humans worried about everything and, at times, were extremely complicated. However, once Turin was safely off the glass surface, he was readily praised for his quick response to his commands. Once again, Turin was filled with a sense of pride regarding his accomplishments. He showed the folks a great Sit on a different surface and an immediate Off when given the command. Life was definitely good for him.

Thoughts of the day's success filled his mind as he attempted to sleep that night. He kept reliving the events from the perfect launch into the air, the targeted stop, the perfect Sit, his immediate response to the Off command given by the folks and the praise that followed. He still didn't know why they seemed so frightened by his demonstration and probably never would. Tomorrow was a new day, and he couldn't wait to return to his glass platform and repeat his launch...only this time, he'd do it better and maybe even faster.

The next day, Turin anxiously ran to the living room so he could duplicate his demonstration from yesterday's success. When he got there, the glass platform was gone. All that was left was a vacant area in the carpet. Perhaps the folks just moved it to a more convenient spot for his launches. This had to be

His glass platform was gone forever.

the reason it was missing. After searching every room in the house, the platform was nowhere to be found and was definitely missing from the house. Disappointment filled his thoughts, but the memory of that moment in time would remain with him forever. His perfect Sit on the glass platform was one of his greatest accomplishments to date. On the other paw, the folks felt a bit differently about his thrilling moment in time. They recalled only the potential for danger and how very lucky their daredevil pup was on that particular day.

As Turin grew older and stronger, he continued to exhibit various types of launches, but none as dangerous as his glass platform launch. His training continued as a potential assistance dog, and he learned his numerous commands quickly. Sit, Stand, Down, and Heel became almost second nature to him. He enjoyed hearing his name and responded promptly when he heard it. Training time was special for him because he would be rewarded with enthusiastic praise when successful. He was learning numerous commands, but the one he enjoyed the most was the Lap command. He couldn't wait to practice that one

Turin loved the Lap command.

because part of the command required just hanging around in position while waiting for his next command. Turin was never one to miss an opportunity for relaxation in between perfecting his jumping skills.

Turin also loved playing with his toys…especially the soft and squeaky ones. As silly and playful as he could be, Turin never shredded or chewed his toys. They were an

endless source of pleasure for him in between training sessions.
While he could be quite
serious at times, he definitely
had a playful side and often
turned his commands into fun-
filled activities. He especially
enjoyed retrieving all sorts of
objects on command, but liked
to inject his sense of humor
whenever he was asked to
retrieve something…even if it
were one of his toys. Whatever

Fun was his middle name!

he did, he did with a sense of playfulness.

While seemingly aloof in the presence of others, Turin
was beginning to demonstrate both a sensitive and intuitive
side. He enjoyed being in the presence of others but wasn't one
to crave attention or cuddle unexpectedly. When he was about
seven months old, he accompanied the folks to a friend's house.
While he didn't know it at the time, his life's direction was
about to change. As he was introduced to the people, he was
very excited to meet them but was especially intrigued by one
of the individuals. She was a beautiful, young woman who
happened to be in a wheel chair. She was waiting for an
assistance dog of her own and was hoping for some good news
about getting one in the near future. This young woman knew
all of the commands in preparation for getting her new partner
and asked if she might try out those commands with Turin.

Having Turin experience hearing his commands given
by someone else was quite beneficial for him, and the folks
were happy to grant the young woman's request. Our dad
handed the leash over to the young woman, and Turin quickly

directed his attention to her. Something about this individual captivated him. Was it the kindness reflected in her eyes or the tenderness shown in her smile that made him want to find out more about her? He didn't quite know, but what he did know was that he had to get to know her better. With Turin's leash in her hand, the young woman gave Turin his Heel command signaling him to move to her left side, and off they went down the hall. She was in total control of him, and he consistently maintained eye contact with her while awaiting further directions. The individuals, who witnessed this behavior, were amazed at Turin's response to her handling of him.

After practicing his commands, the two of them returned to the main room. Turin looked like quite the professional assistance dog while sitting next to her, and the young woman just beamed with joy having shared this experience with him. As a final command, she gave Turin his Lap command which meant that he was to lay on her lap until otherwise directed. Turin did exactly what he was trained to do, but he didn't stop there. Sensing the young woman's kind-heartedness, he slowly and ever so gently laid his head on her shoulder as if to thank her for the shared experience. He never demonstrated this type of sensitivity to anyone before, yet something so very special about this young woman brought out that intuitive side in him. The adults in the room were stunned by Turin's behavior. Needless to say, not a dry eye remained in the room as a few people reached for tissues to wipe the tears of happiness from their eyes. That simple act of kindness on Turin's part changed his legacy and would be remembered for years to come. Sure, he still attempted some reckless stunts, but he also found a new direction for his life.

Assistance to others became a real possibility for him as well as a goal in the years to come.

Turin had a new beginning, and his public outings became more frequent and varied in terms of locations. Now that he knew all of his commands and walked nicely on his leash, he wasn't just walking around the neighborhood or visiting the park. He was all dressed up in his working gear and ready to go out into the real world. Turin was representing his organization and was taking this responsibility very seriously. He wasn't sure where he would go, but he knew that it would be an adventure. Our dad took him on his very first, grown-up public outing, and the two of them went off to explore the world together. On that particular day, they became a team.

From that day on, Turin and our dad went on daily excursions to various places of interest. Each day was more exciting than the previous one. They became regulars at the Sunday morning church service and as tempting as the clear water in that Holy Water Fountain was, Turin only thought about taking a drink. They walked in both indoor and outdoor malls while gazing at the stores, greeted some children, rode up and down in the glass

Now they were a team!

elevators and rested at the Food Courts. Turin, while situated under the table in the Food Courts, kept himself occupied by searching for chewing gum stuck to the underside of the table tops. Much to the dismay of our dad, Turin was always successful in finding that one bit of gum stuck to the underside of a table. Getting gum out of Turin's mouth and whiskers was a bit difficult, but that inconvenience didn't seem to bother Turin. So as not to be caught, he waited until our dad's attention was elsewhere. Then, he'd quietly and carefully examine the underside of the table. If even the tiniest bit of gum were there, he'd definitely find it and have a fast chew. He didn't seem to care if gum clung to his whiskers or teeth. To him, searching for gum was just a game to occupy his time while under the table. Let's face it...it wasn't exactly the best seat in the house. Once in a while, they went to fancy restaurants, but Turin wasn't able to find any gum under those tables. Table cloths usually hid any remnants of sticky items. Turin didn't care because the fun was in the hopes of finding something. I have to give him credit...that pup sure knew how to have a good time.

Turin and our dad also represented their organization at fund raisers such as gift wrapping events, presentations in pet stores and even some dog walks. Turin enjoyed the dog walks the best because he could see other dogs working toward a career in service as well as dogs who had already graduated and were with their partners. Participating in the dog walks was a lot of fun but quite

Dog walks were the most fun.

tiresome. When he got home, he welcomed the opportunity to get some well-deserved rest. Sometimes the folks even allowed him to sleep on the couch as a reward for appropriate public behavior. While the couch was usually forbidden territory, it was his favorite place to sleep.

Z z z z z z z z z z

Turin had more unique adventures in the months to come during his training for assistance. One time in particular, he and another assistance dog in training slipped out of their collars and got loose in an outdoor shopping mall. They had such great fun running around after each other while their leashes flew like kite strings in the air...much to the amusement of onlookers but to the overall dismay of their handlers. That certainly wasn't the best behavior for assistance dogs in training...especially goofing off in front of so many people while wearing their training capes. Both dogs knew full well that consequences were forthcoming, but that didn't deter them from enjoying their momentary frivolity. When the fun ended, they felt that their penalties might be lessened since they did come back when called and neither of them jumped into the huge water fountain in the middle of the mall. In their minds, those positive behaviors had to count for something. What were those pups thinking?

Turin went on to have many more adventures with our family, but he never really knew what an influence he had on them and on the puppies that followed in his paw steps. While fostering Turin was the folks' first attempt at raising a potential assistance dog, what they didn't know at the time, was that their experience with him wouldn't be their last. For them, it was just the beginning of adventures that would span well over fourteen enjoyable years...all because of their first experience with Turin.

The adventure started with Turin.

The young puppies that followed in his lead as potential assistance dogs entered the sorority house as energetic whippersnappers, and after twelve to fifteen months of adventures, they left as well-prepared dogs who were most eager to enter the next chapter in their exciting lives...advanced training. Their roller coaster rides of canine adventures were only possible because of the impact that Turin's residency had on his foster family. This continuation of canine adventures in the sorority house became Turin's enduring legacy.

Turin definitely had some fun times while at the sorority house, and only a few of his adventures were shared today. While there are many more stories to come, those tales are saved for another time, another place and another photo on the Wall of Fame...

Off to Advanced Training

Kessen

While I really enjoyed sharing some of Turin's adventures, I'm now focused on the pictures of Kessen...our respected pack leader and the second dog who was raised by our foster family for assistance. Looking at the various photos of him on the wall, I decide upon the one that contains a few poses...each depicting a different side of his personality and a variety of stories. As a beginner in the storytelling business, I hope to tell the stories as Kessen intended them to be told...especially since these stories are all about him.

As the canine pack leader in the sorority house, his position necessitated seriousness at all times, but that didn't always happen. When I first met Kessen, I thought he was a bit pompous and totally inflexible in terms of rules and regulations. However, after sharing some time with him as an adult canine, I realized how very wrong I was. My views of him changed considerably. I came to understand that his journey was one of challenges, disappointments and successes that he, himself, chose to willingly share with me as part of his legacy as the neighborhood storyteller. I was filled with pride that he

45

had chosen me out of every member of the pack for this awesome duty.

Kessen wasn't always the stern taskmaster as demonstrated by his early puppyhood days. Traveling as a puppy from sunny California to the harsh winter of the Midwest was a great challenge for him. It was his first experience with snow, wind and sleet. Never in his short life had he experienced such weather. The worst weather that he'd ever seen in California was a bit of a rain shower that only lasted a few minutes, and that shower usually ended with a colorful rainbow in the distance. This weather was entirely different and not at all pleasant.

Arriving at the regional center in Ohio, his thin puppy coat was not at all prepared for the harsh Midwest winter. However, his foster mother shielded him from the cold by wrapping him in a soft, sweet-smelling blanket and holding him closely in her lap all the way home from the center. Once he was in his new home, he was still somewhat disoriented. He

Kessen felt so alone.

missed his biological mother who taught him to be a brave, strong, independent and adventurous pup. But now, those lessons seemed forgotten as he was entirely on his own...without the comfort of his mother and his siblings. Although this new place was welcoming and warm, he still felt lonely and afraid. His sister Kelyn, who was his best friend, went to a place called North Carolina, but he didn't know where the others went. He just knew that he was alone in this new house and hoped that someday he'd meet his sister once again. At that very moment, nothing seemed possible.

His first days in the new home were very difficult since he was missing his family so much, but his new family tried to make him feel at home. They played with him a lot, and at night, his new foster mother even took time to sing a special song to him. According to her song, he was her *sunshine,* but he really didn't know what that meant. He only knew that her soft lingering tones lulled him to sleep. Years later, Kessen found out that she sang the same song to all of the puppies when they first arrived at the sorority house. Knowing that fact didn't change anything because when she sang for him, he felt safe and special. As far as he was concerned, that was all that mattered.

I will briefly interrupt this story to let you, the reader, know that when I was just a puppy and new to the sorority house, I, too, thought that I was our mom's only *sunshine*. Truth be told, I was a bit disillusioned when I first heard Kessen tell that story because I believed that I was our mom's one and only special puppy. The more I thought about it, the more I realized that our individual personalities made us shine in our own way, and our mom's singing just reinforced that belief. Still, Mom sure had a lot of *sunshines* over the years, yet she made each of us feel as if she were singing just for us. Her song and her belief in each of us was such an extraordinary gift, and we, in turn, never got tired of hearing her voice.

Getting back to the story…In time, Kessen stopped howling in the middle of the night and started enjoying a bit of freedom offered to him in his play area. While he still missed his biological mother and siblings, he was beginning to like this new family. They, in turn, really seemed to care for him in a special way. He wasn't sure what to call these folks because he didn't want to diminish his love for his biological mother, yet referring to them as his foster folks didn't seem right either. Sammy, the Golden Retriever who lived next door, helped him through that conflict by sharing all the right reasons for calling them mom and dad, and his reasoning convinced Kessen that

it was the right thing to do. It was a bit awkward at first, but he'd get used to it. Kessens's new life was certainly looking brighter and brighter with each passing day.

In a short period of time, Kessen followed a daily routine of eating, playing, more training and sleeping. Playing in the snow was one of his favorite things to do once

Snow Baby

he got used to it because the snow felt crisp and cool on the pads of his paws. He was also quite inquisitive, and being a young puppy, he enjoyed this new world that presented surprises on a daily basis. He never saw or heard birds before nor did he ever see a squirrel or a chipmunk. Now these sights and unusual sounds were everyday happenings. Noticing a chipmunk disappear into a flower barrel really intrigued him, and he couldn't wait to explore the depths of that container the first chance he got. He never found the chipmunk when he

He was very inquisitive.

had the chance to look into the container, but at least his curiosity was satisfied.

In addition to his play time, Kessen also spent time training for possible assistance. He didn't know what that even meant, but he got to wear a special cape when working on his commands and received treats for his hard work. His training time became dress-up experiences filled with fun and treats. As he got a bit older and saw other dogs wearing their capes in the training class, Kessen thought those capes just

His cape had magical powers.

might be magical because all of the dogs knew their commands when they wore them. Since people smiled at him when he was wearing his cape, Kessen was convinced that the cape unquestionably had mysterious powers. Was he serious? To be honest, I was amazed that Kessen even shared that little kibble of information with me. Somehow, I never thought of him as having such an imaginative side to his personality, and yet he definitely lived up to that aspect with his magical cape theory. Nevertheless, I must put a temporary hold on my editorializing and get back to the business of storytelling.

As time passed, Kessen enjoyed the last bit of snow in the yard while continuing to do some silly things. Upon seeing his friend Sammy in the next yard and wanting to greet him, Kessen rushed through the yard toward the fence but overestimated his speed as well as his ability to stop at the fence line. He ran right into the fence at full speed and got his head caught between the fence rails. Unable to free his head from the confining rails, he howled and flailed around in a panic. Seeing what had happened, our mom rushed over to the fence, calmed him with her soothing voice and freed him from his unfortunate confinement. Needless to say, he never did that again. While he certainly did some silly things, he was simply engaging in typical puppy antics. However, this event was yet another surprising bit of information shared by our esteemed pack leader. He was being amazingly candid about his puppy days and not at all fearful of appearing ridiculous. As far as I was concerned, this type of sharing took real depth of character. In my mind, he was more than just the pack leader...he was, by virtue of being himself, the total package!

Kessen admitted to doing some very foolish things as a puppy. He once thought that the baby pool in the yard was a huge water bowl placed there for his refreshment. After having a good laugh, Sammy clued him in on the misconception. Once Kessen realized that the pool wasn't a water bowl at all, he'd drop his rubber balls into the water and attempt to grab them. This wasn't much fun since he spent a good deal of time gulping water, and the balls were just too slippery to grasp.

His plan worked!

Eventually, he decided to empty the water from the baby pool. By doing that, he could grab the rubber balls without gulping water. That idea really worked and proved to him that he did occasionally have some good ideas. It did, however, take some strategizing and a good deal of time for him to come up with the idea...but, not before he swallowed a lot of water.

As Kessen got older, he developed faster planning and decision-making techniques. All types of skills were taught at the sorority house, and the dogs in training were required to pick up their toys each night before going to bed. Teaching them to do that was relatively easy and was accomplished by offering a small reward in exchange for any toy left on the floor. The reward wasn't known until the toy was retrieved and placed in either our mom's or dad's left hand. Doing this would signal the opening of the other hand to reveal the hidden reward. Kessen's love of food resulted in his reaching the highest level of proficiency in terms of trading toys. He'd bring one toy at a time to our mom or dad and get some type of reward in the form of a treat for each item retrieved. The value of the reward wasn't entirely a consideration for him because it was food, and according to him, as long as it was food, it was worth the effort to retrieve the toy.

Until one day, his standard of retrieval-reward changed. When it was toy retrieval time, he brought one of his rubber bones that he found on the sunroom floor to our mom. As he put the bone in her left hand, he then gently took the treat offered from her right hand. The generous food gods certainly smiled on him because his reward was a tender bit of poached chicken, and that was one

Delicious Treat Day

of his favorite treats. Knowing that a high level of treat was being traded that evening, he ran to get another toy. This time, he chose a squeak toy left under the dining room table. Once again, he repeated the process only this time he went to our dad and received a morsel of dried liver...another prized reward from the treat collection. By this time, Kessen was on a mission for dropped toys, and after searching all of the rooms, he spotted a tennis ball lodged under a chair. He struggled and stretched his body as far as he could to retrieve that ball. Treats were on his mind, and nothing would stop him from getting that ball. It was the only toy left on the floor in the entire house and was his last chance for getting a special reward. Once he was able to push the ball from under the chair with his paw, he grasped it tightly in his mouth and ran to the kitchen as fast as he could to make the final trade of the day. By this time, his mouth watered in his anticipation of what treasure lurked in the palm of our parent's hands. It could be another morsel of dried liver or a piece of that delicious poached chicken. Maybe it was something of an even higher level of treasure, and in his mind, the food possibilities were endless. Racing to the kitchen, Kessen rushed to our dad with his tennis ball. As Dad held out his hand, Kessen gently placed the ball into the palm of his outstretched hand. As if on cue, our dad opened the fingers of his other hand to expose yet another treasured item. At first, Kessen didn't recognize what it was because it certainly wasn't poached chicken and definitely wasn't dried liver. Instead, it was a tidbit that was orange in color and a bit oval-shaped. Kessen was positive that he had never eaten anything that looked like that in the past, but up until this moment, he hadn't been selective with edible items. He reached over, sniffed the item and looked inquisitively at our dad. Dad smiled and told him that it was a carrot…a very healthy treat. Kessen, not really understanding what healthy meant, took another sniff, looked up at our dad and then took his tennis ball back from our dad's other hand. While Kessen chose to forfeit his final treat for the day, he discovered that he did, indeed, have standards of treat appreciation.

As it turned out, every day was a learning experience for Kessen…even in the food department. In the end, he learned to enjoy healthy foods in the form of cooked vegetables mixed in with his daily meals. Eventually, he even decided that carrots weren't so bad after all and in not taking the carrot during that one evening of retrieval-reward exercises, he missed out on an extremely tasty reward.

Not all of Kessen's training revolved around food and playing games. As time passed, he was required to learn some serious commands for his role as a potential assistance dog. When Kessen was only nine months old, he had his first opportunity to put one of his commands to good use by lending assistance to someone in need. Now, he knew a number of commands, but still wasn't sure what assistance was all about. On this particular day, he and our mom were taking their usual walk around the neighborhood. Flowers of all sorts were now in bloom, and their fragrances filled the air as they walked past the houses. The trees were no longer bare but instead were full of leaves of all shapes and sizes. It was spring, and life was good…at least for the moment.

Without any warning whatsoever, his life dramatically changed. Mom tripped on a crack in the pavement and fell to the ground. Even though she dropped his leash, Kessen knew that he had to stay with her, and he could tell that she had a lot of pain in both her hand and ankle. Not knowing what to do and becoming more frightened by the moment, he instinctively moved closer to her in an effort to offer some comfort. As she attempted to get up, Kessen could see that she was not going to be able to accomplish this by herself. He still didn't know what he could do, but our mom did. She gave him his Stand command. At first, he wasn't sure what to do, but then he remembered that Stand meant to brace his legs in a standing position similar to a show dog's stance when being examined by a judge. When he did this, our mom, using her good hand, was able to support herself on his sturdy body as a means of getting to her feet. With Kessen now confidently lending support and comfort by her side, she was able to hobble over to a neighbor's house for assistance.

Luckily their neighbor, who was at home and grasped what had happened, immediately prepared an ice pack for our mom's hand to prevent further swelling. Feelings of relief

Today he helped someone in need.

swept over Kessen as our dad arrived to take Mom to the hospital. The neighbor was kind enough to take Kessen home while Dad was helping our mother. Once at home, the realization of what had really happened and the part that he had played in the outcome caused Kessen's body to momentarily tremble. He had actually helped someone in need, and that is what his training was all about. As Kessen began to relax, the trembling subsided, and exhaustion overcame him. Hours later, our mom came home from the hospital using crutches for her injured ankle and a cast on her hand. Seeing her in that condition rekindled that sense of responsibility in Kessen for his role in helping her. He liked that feeling and for the very first time,

Kessen knew exactly what he wanted to do with his life. It was all about service to others. Kessen's act of heroism on that day earned him the extra-special nickname of K-Man. Every time his folks called him that, it reminded him of the help he gave to someone in need that resulted in such a change in his life's ambition.

On the other paw, it wasn't all serious work and training for Kessen. He went on a variety of adventures while he was in training. Together with our mom and dad, they gave numerous presentations regarding the role of assistance dogs at the high school. At first, they'd enter the building when classes were in session so Kessen could get used to the slippery floors and ceiling lights that illuminated spots on the floors. Some dogs jumped at those spots on the floors, but Kessen didn't mind them at all. He also had the opportunity to walk up stairs that had openings between the rails. Going up the stairs to the second floor was a bit scary, but each time they went up those stairs, it became easier and easier to do it. After his second trip, he didn't notice the spaces between the rails at all.

Mom shared information with the classes about the role of assistance dogs as well as the intense training involved with their preparation for service. Dad talked about the need for volunteers at various fund raisers and provided opportunities for students to get involved with the assistance program. Kessen's job was to demonstrate his knowledge of numerous basic commands. The students really enjoyed seeing him walk backwards, respond to commands given in a whisper, and they especially liked his turning off the classroom lights with his paw. Learning the correct way to greet a dog was also part of the presentation, and each student had the opportunity to greet Kessen. He enjoyed that part of the presentation the best.

Soon, their presentations were in demand, and he and the folks gave seventeen demonstrations in three weeks to the various classes. Because he was used to the facility, Kessen was now entering the high school while the halls were bustling with students, lockers were clanging and the pep band was playing in the auditorium. At first, he foolishly thought the pep band was playing just for him when he entered the school. But, he later found out they were really preparing for the football game scheduled for that evening. Because he was having such a good time at the high school, that bit of information didn't bother Kessen at all. Students welcomed him by name and eagerly lined up just to greet him. He definitely was a star on the high school scene. Once again, Kessen was in his glory!

Following the high school presentations, Kessen and the folks were invited to do additional presentations for various clubs and organizations. Some were given in parks, at dog walks and even in churches. The pastor of one particular church hoped to raise additional funds to ensure easier access for the disabled of her church community and requested a presentation dedicated to that goal. Our mom and dad were more than willing to help, so they all visited the church for this special presentation.

When they got there, Mom was really enthusiastic because one of the church elders equipped her with this incredible head-set microphone. Kessen could tell our mom felt magical, and she wasn't even wearing a cape! Anyway, Kessen had developed a distinct pattern of attention-getting mischief during presentations by attempting to untie our mom's shoe laces while she spoke. Because our mom was prepared for this, she asked the congregation to ignore Kessen's attempt at attention-getting if he started to chew on her shoe laces during the presentation.

Soon after she began her presentation, Kessen began his efforts to untie those double-tied shoe laces. In spite of our mom's instructions, the congregation couldn't help themselves and laughed at Kessen's attempts. Kessen was overjoyed at the attention, and much to his surprise, Mom even joined in the laughter along with the others. While our mom might have corrected Kessen, she realized that he, along with the congregation, was just having a good time. As a follow up, the pastor eventually got the funding for changes that led to improved access for the disabled members. However, in future presentations, our mom was shrewd enough to wear shoes without laces. Her tool box of training techniques was always expanding. She was no longer a first-time puppy raiser, but one who anticipated as well as prepared for any situation.

One of Kessen's most memorable experiences was the family's trip across the country via scenic Route 66 to sunny California and back. While positioned in the back section of their station wagon known as Sparky 2, Kessen was able

California Dreamer

to see all of the sights of the countryside as the family traveled to their destination. He enjoyed the view of the mountains in Colorado, the activity in LasVegas along the memorable strip seen from the highway, the deserts filled with various forms of cacti that lined the highway as well as the stunning views of the Santa Rosa Mountains that surrounded the family's time share in Palm Desert, California. Our mom surprised Kessen and our dad by learning how to play the harmonica while traveling. According to her, that musical endeavor would not only pass the time but would also add entertainment to the journey. By the time they reached California, she was able to play a somewhat identifiable version of *The Battle Hymn of the Republic* as well as a rather unique rendition of *Taps*. Everything else just sounded the same and, at times, wasn't very enjoyable. But, they were captives in the car and had no alternative way to get to California.

The family eventually got to their destination with their ability to distinguish sounds intact. Their time share was located in a luxurious area of the desert that offered all the amenities of a five-star hotel. There were numerous pools, saunas, tennis courts, music for pool-side entertainment, exercise areas, shops and restaurants. It was a little city unto itself, and Kessen was loving every moment of their vacation.

They visited numerous tourist sights, ate at all kinds of restaurants and went to a windmill farm with acres of pin-wheeled shaped structures that filled the landscape as far as his eyes could see. A visit to a date farm was next on their traveling agenda, and Kessen had his own special reasons for wanting to go there. In his mind, a date farm was just the right place to meet females of the canine persuasion. His hackles bristled with excitement as they approached their destination. Upon arriving and seeing that it was actually a place that grew and sold dates, his enthusiasm quickly turned to disappointment. This particular date farm wasn't a place to meet females at all. Nevertheless, sulking wasn't going to change anything and moping around wasn't going to make female canines appear in the middle of the date fields. So, Kessen ended the pity party with his decision to make the most of it and just have a good time.

During the vacation, the days were filled with early morning walks around the tree-lined grounds, visits to street fairs, leisurely strolls down glamorous El Paseo Drive with its high end shops, hikes in the mountains as well as peaceful relaxation time around the numerous pools located within the boundaries of the property. It was the perfect vacation for the entire family.

After a wonderful week spent in such luxury, they began their long journey home. However, their pleasant vacation memories were shattered just outside the city of Albuquerque, New Mexico when an eighteen wheeler truck lost its drive shaft on the highway in front of them. Something that looked like a huge log bounced around the highway and posed a definite threat to their safety. What turned out to be the truck's drive shaft bounced beneath Sparky 2, ripped its way to freedom under the car and then took chunks out of the tire rims causing the back tires to burst. Once freed from the underside of the car, this bouncing projectile then continued on its way and blew out the tires on the car traveling behind them. The folks could actually see the highway through the ripped portion of the car's floor. Amidst the smoke and scent of burning tires, our dad was able to maneuver Sparky 2 safely to the side of the road. While everyone was thoroughly shaken but unharmed in the accident, the cost of what happened in terms of human and canine emotions was great. Everyone, including Kessen, was totally frightened by the accident, but they were convinced that their Guardian Angels were with them on the road at that moment in time for all of them to be unharmed in the accident.

Because of his foolish attempt to get into the front seat of the car with the folks, Kessen just happened to be crated in his canvas kennel at the time of the accident. If not for his earlier foolishness, he might not have been crated and might have been seriously hurt in the accident. While the entire family was safe, unfortunately, Sparky 2 was wrecked. Sadly, it had to be shipped home on a flatbed trailer and wasn't able to be repaired. Because of the lack of availability of a rental car, the family spent the weekend in a crowded motel room. On Monday, when a car was available, they resumed their journey in a rented SUV. As far as Kessen was concerned, it definitely wasn't Sparky 2 but was a pretty comfortable car. Besides, he could sleep anywhere…anytime!

The family continued their travels along Route 66 and stopped at a quaint motel in a very small town somewhere along the Texas border. According to Kessen, the night sky was as dark as velvet, and the stars shone like diamonds in the sky. He had never seen such dramatic stars in his life. In spite of the turmoil of the accident, that sky and those stars would forever remain a pleasant picture in his mind.

They resumed their journey bright and early the next morning, and after driving most of the day, the folks decided to stay overnight at a hotel close to the famous St. Louis Arch. That structure, in itself, was an awesome sight to see but not as exciting as the potential of reaching their destination. Tomorrow, they would be home at last. The trip was definitely a memorable one in Kessen's adventures while in training, but his getting home was even better.

Kessen only had a few more weeks left before he'd have to leave the sorority house and report to advanced training. Our folks had a special treat in store for each of the dogs before going to advanced training called a Canine Fun Swim. The nearby hydrotherapy center offered times for healthy dogs to enjoy swimming in an actual swimming pool. Kessen loved water and was ecstatic over the possibility of that type of experience. To date, his only pool experience was wading in his baby pool in the back yard, and that, in itself, was even quite shallow compared to the water used when he was given a bath. This impending pool experience was the real deal as far as he was concerned.

Once the family arrived at the hydrotherapy center, they walked a short distance to the pool house. Kessen was fitted with a special life-vest that had handles on it so that he'd always be protected in case he ran into trouble in the water. As a safety precaution, pool assistants positioned themselves on either side of him as he made his way down a ramp into the cool water. Kessen was not frightened at all while going down the ramp and just enjoyed the feeling of the water flowing over

Kessen loved to swim.

and around his body as he descended into the pool. It was such a glorious feeling, and one that he had never experienced. As soon as the pool assistants realized that he was safe in the water by himself, they let him go off on his own to chase water toys that had been thrown into the water. Using his feathered tail as a rudder, Kessen sailed effortlessly through the water with a toy bone in his mouth. Our mom and dad took pictures of him as he swam back and forth with various toys in his mouth. When his swim time was over, he reluctantly came up the ramp and out of the water. Our folks were so happy that Kessen thoroughly enjoyed their special gift of swimming in an actual pool but later realized that there was such a thing as too much of a good time.

That night, Kessen was quite restless and couldn't seem to relax enough to sleep. He paced from room to room in the house, and our folks weren't quite sure how to help him. In the morning, they noticed that not only was he not enthusiastic about his morning meal, but his tail had gone limp as well. Usually, the prospect of his morning meal brought on great waves of energetic tail-wagging but not on this particular morning. Something was definitely wrong with him, and our folks decided to take him to the animal hospital. When they got there, even the receptionists at the animal hospital noticed Kessen's limp tail and sad expression. His tail usually wagged constantly when he visited because he was so happy to see them, but his tail was in no condition to wag today.

Within a few minutes, the veterinarian came into the exam room and thoroughly examined Kessen…especially the position of his tail. It was the veterinarian's very first experience with this type of ailment, and he recognized it immediately as a condition called Limber Tail Syndrome. Since Kessen swam so enthusiastically the day before while using his strong Retriever tail as a rudder, he strained the muscles in his tail which, in turn, caused the limpness and discomfort. It was similar to an individual who strained a muscle while overdoing exercise. Kessen didn't understand that at all. He just never knew that having so much fun could be harmful. A few days of antibiotics diminished the discomfort as well as allowed his tail to resume its typical wagging ability. In spite of his distress,

Kessen would not have traded that pool experience for anything.

Two weeks later, Kessen's training time with our family came to an end, and he was now prepared for his entrance into Advanced Training or Puppy College as it was affectionately called. He was anxious to begin this new chapter in his life even though it meant leaving the family. He would certainly miss them, but assistance to someone in need was his goal in life. Before his journey ended with them and his new chapter in life began, Kessen went to church with the family for the last time and shared their tradition of having each dog blessed by their favorite priest. Since he and the family went to the church service every Sunday, Kessen knew the priest very well and was anxious to see him. However, this time was particularly special because it was the last time that they would see each other. The priest looked lovingly at Kessen while blessing him, and even the folks got teary eyed at the reality of Kessen's leaving. However, Kessen, being the rascal that he was, brought laughter to the situation by attempting to take a drink of water from the Holy Water Fountain. He always had to have the last laugh! He was now fully prepared, body and soul, for advanced training.

Soon after his arrival, Kessen learned that not all dogs wanted to be of assistance to others, and not all dogs could be successful in that career…even if they wanted it for themselves. Kessen truly wanted an assistance career, but his sensitive temperament just couldn't handle the stress of the kennel environment. While he worked well in the training areas, he couldn't handle the pressure of the kennels. Losing six pounds in sixteen days took a toll on him, and it was clear that he just wasn't adapting to kennel life. For the sake of his health, the organization released Kessen from the service program. It was a very sad day for Kessen.

Upon hearing the news, our mom and dad rushed to the facility to adopt him as their own family member. Seeing him in such a sad and sickly state was devastating to them, and they cried off and on most of the way home. For the first time in a few weeks, Kessen slept soundly in the back seat of the car while wrapped in our mom's sweatshirt. Surrounded by her comforting scent, he felt safe and was finally going home!

As soon as our mom and dad got him home, their challenges involved restoring Kessen's health which took six weeks of treating colitis and over six months of dealing with his sleeping in corners. The advanced training environment had such a devastating effect on him, and it didn't just affect his health either. That career of assistance was what he wanted more than anything, and the sadness that he felt over the loss of that opportunity haunted him.

Once his health was restored and recognizing how much he enjoyed helping others, our mom and dad enrolled Kessen in an animal-assisted therapy program. Our dad would be his partner, and both of them would learn new skills and have the opportunity to help others in group settings. Just because he wasn't cut out to assist one individual didn't mean he couldn't help in other ways. This new gig with our dad would still be a form of service, and that was all that mattered to him

Among other things, and there were a lot of things to learn for assisted therapy work, Kessen learned how to approach people in wheelchairs, greet individuals who were using walkers and even walk next to people on crutches. It just wasn't proper or safe for a dog to flop on someone's lap while they were in a wheel chair or get the leash tangled in crutches. This type of behavior was just unacceptable. There was so much to learn, but Kessen was convinced that this program was meant for him. He especially enjoyed having our dad as his partner.

Games were also an important part of his training, and he learned all sorts of ways to amuse children including puzzles, brain games, bowling games, jump ropes, ring tosses, and he received lots and lots of treats…usually a green bean or a piece of hot dog taken from a plastic fork. Children didn't get frightened if they fed a dog from a plastic fork since the dog's whiskers didn't tickle their hands, and the dog still got the treat. It was a win-win situation. As he progressed through the program, Kessen's self-confidence grew, and he was back in the game of helping others.

Once he completed his training program, Kessen and our dad were ready for their first assignment. Tension was high as Kessen waited for what might be something he could do for the rest of his life to help others. He just couldn't wait to get started, and he sure didn't have to wait very long. Going back to school was his first official assignment. He and our dad were going to work with two different

He was ready to work.

groups of children in classroom settings. The first group just happened to be children in wheelchairs, and Kessen was prepared for this assignment. He learned his lesson while in training when he landed in the person's lap on his first attempt at a greeting to someone in a wheel chair. The trainers were quick to demonstrate the correct form of greeting, and Kessen learned that greetings could be polite without the lap-launch approach. His excitement just got the best of him on that first try. Anyway, he was thoroughly prepared now and raring to go. Those children were definitely safe from his enthusiastic lap-launch!

The children were so excited to see him, and the first thing they did was take Kessen for a walk. Using a specially made double leash, the child held one handle of the leash while our dad held the other. The child's aide pushed the wheel chair while all of them passed through the halls of the school. Kessen was thrilled because he was finally doing what he was trained to do. That first walk down the hall with the child holding his leash was a moment that he would always treasure. Once they returned to the classroom, the next child would do the same. Each child had the opportunity to walk Kessen through the halls.

The next thing that they did was to feed Kessen with the plastic fork. Squeals of laughter were heard as Kessen gently took a treat from each child's fork. Brushing him came next and gave the children a bit of exercise, while Kessen, in turn, received numerous massages! It was a win-win situation for all! His first visit went very well, and Kessen couldn't wait until the next scheduled visit with the children.

The next classroom had a group of autistic children who wanted to play games with him. Their favorite game was the Bowling Game which happened to be Kessen's favorite as well. The children placed a long mat resembling a bowling alley lane on the floor. It had a triangular section of colorful circles at the very end, and each circle contained a number. Styrofoam bowling pins were placed on the circles, and the game was ready to begin. At the opposite end of the mat was a huge Styrofoam bowling ball. On the count of three, they all yelled "Kessen, Go Bowling!" Upon hearing those words, Kessen excitedly pushed the ball down the lane into the pins in an attempt to knock as many of them down as he could. The children applauded, and then counted the number of pins that fell and identified the colors of the circles. They were learning as well as having fun. They did this a few times, and sometimes Kessen would really get them excited by grabbing one of the pins and running around the room. He wasn't supposed to do this, but he really liked to clown around once in a while. Our dad was not at all pleased with this breech in classroom etiquette, but the children loved it and squealed with laughter as Kessen circled the room Their excited responses to his shenanigans only encouraged him to do it again. After playing a few more games, Kessen and our dad had to leave. The children cheered and waved as the therapy team left the classroom. On their next visit, there would be more games and definitely more fun. Kessen was doing what he loved to do…making children happy.

His next gig was the library reading program which turned out to be tremendous fun for Kessen. He was part of a Four Dog Team. Children signed up to read to a dog of their choice for fifteen minutes on six consecutive Saturdays. There was a dog and handler in each of the four corners of the room with a blanket laid out for the child's comfort. The child would select his favorite dog and spend time reading to his new buddy. The handler's only role was to hold the leash and never interfere. It was just the child and the dog spending some enjoyable time together. While petting Kessen, some children described the pictures in the book to him as they read, and some even brought travel brochures to show him as they read about their vacation travels. At times, a child might be a bit skeptical of being with a big dog and would sit at the farthest corner of the blanket when starting to read. However, by the end of the reading time, the child would be right next to Kessen with one hand wrapped around him and the other holding the book. It was a wonderful program, and Kessen just loved being a part of something so very special.

Kessen told me a number of stories about himself, and the ones that showed his happy-go-lucky behaviors were the most surprising to me. Being the pack leader and staunch supporter of rules and regulations, it wasn't often that I saw the impish side of him or even imagined that it existed. But, this carefree aspect of his personality did exist, and his stories were often verified by members of the canine community.

While participating in an agility class a few years ago, Kessen was in line to win the first prize in a special competition. He accurately negotiated the obstacles on the agility course with speed and tenacity. But, just short of the advance to the final platform, Kessen's silliness got the best of him. Seeing the towel under the seesaw that protected the board from bouncing when the dogs traversed it was too much of a temptation for him. To the audience it was just a towel, but to Kessen, it was a victory flag. He grabbed that towel and circled the course with the towel flying high in the air. Needless to say, it took our mom's standing in the middle of the course with her hands on her hips to get him to stop taking those imaginary victory laps. Kessen relinquished his victory flag, generically identified as a towel, to our mom and knew that consequences were soon to follow. The folks, somewhat embarrassed by his playful behavior in such a prestigious competition, quickly left and never returned to that facility again. However, once they got into their car, they had a good laugh about it on the ride home!

But, the story doesn't end with that incident. Somehow a rumor circulated among the canine members of the facility that the agility gods were angered by Kessen's self-serving actions. Because of what he did, his canine spirit was condemned to haunt the training facility...especially the agility course for all eternity. There, his spirit would continue to haunt the dogs who followed in his paw steps. The rumor quickly spread from dog to dog in the training facility. Soon, dogs reported seeing Kessen's clouded face in the material of the closed tunnel on the agility course, and other competitors even

Was it really just a rumor?

heard muffled howling while in the darkened tunnel. Because some dogs believed the rumors to be true, they refused to enter the closed tunnel...resulting in loss of points. Noticing that towel positioned under the plank of the seesaw made it all the more frightening for some of the dogs in the competition. Of course, not all of the dogs believed in the legend, and those who did wouldn't readily brag about their belief. However, even the bravest of dogs experienced just a hint of apprehension when approaching the closed tunnel or seeing that towel used as Kessen's victory flag. In one playful escapade, Kessen became a legend on the agility course.

When Kessen told me this story, I was amazed not just because of the story, but because he chose to even tell me about it. Here was our responsible and respectful pack leader savoring the fact that he became a legend due to playful behavior. I'll tell you this, dear readers, he sure had some surprises for me in terms of his experiences.

I was learning that Kessen had many facets to his personality. While on a break from the animal-assisted therapy programs, Kessen went on a family trip to Charlotte, North Carolina and was reunited with his sister Kelyn. Her foster parents became friends with Kessen's folks via the internet when the pups were in training, and they planned a trip to meet and reunite the dogs. The trip to Charlotte was exciting and meeting his sister again was a dream come true for Kessen.

They spent the weekend getting to know all about each other's lives and shared all kinds of stories about themselves. Kelyn lived with four other dogs, so every day was an adventure for her. She, too, was a therapy dog and enjoyed helping others. They had so much in common…especially their love of water. Kelyn truly enjoyed hearing about his limber tail episode following his strenuous swimming pool experience. They were so comfortable together as if they were never separated. Soon it was time to leave, but both Kessen and Kelyn had this

Sweet Sister Kelyn

wonderful memory to keep with them for the rest of their lives. While they might not be together, they had their family bond, and no one could ever take that away from them.

Following their trip to Charlotte, the family continued their travels to the seashore. They rented a beach house on Topsail Island that was located off the coast of North Carolina. Their house was right on the beach and in direct proximity to the ocean. Kessen was off the charts in terms of excitement. He had been in swimming pools before, but he had never seen the ocean and never dreamt that he'd ever swim in it. It was a bit scary at first because of the way the waves came crashing on to

This was one big swimming pool!

the shore, but Kessen soon got used to their movements. He was in his glory thrashing around in the cool water and dodging the waves. Soon, he was thoroughly soaked, but loving every minute of it...so much so, that when he finally came out of the water, his tail was a bit sore. As night time came, he was in a good deal of pain, and his tail wasn't working properly. Instead of being able to wag it, his tail just drooped down towards the floor. Once again, Limber Tail Syndrome reared its ugly head, or should I say reared its ugly tail?

Kessen had forgotten that he had injured his tail a long time ago following the Canine Fun Swim at the hydrotherapy center. He did the same thing again, only this time the ocean was his swimming pool. Nevertheless, our mom remembered the tail incident when packing for the trip to the beach and brought his medication just in case he repeated the same behavior in the ocean. Sure enough, he did just what our mom thought he would do when he swam in the ocean. Among his many attributes, Kessen was, at times, somewhat predictable when it came to having fun.

That night as Kessen was sprawled on the deck listening to the waves crashing along the shore, the folks knew that while Kessen felt uncomfortable, he'd probably do it all over again the next day if precautions weren't in place. To avoid

Water Buddies

another painful incident, our dad attached a tether to Kessen's collar and accompanied him into the water. These precautions not only ensured Kessen's safety, but also kept his tail in mint condition.

Since I was the newly-chosen keeper of the facts and interim-storyteller in Kessen's absence, I found that even

sharing his adventures made me laugh. His stories came to life in ways that I never imagined possible. He seemed like a typical canine…one who got into silly predicaments, made mistakes and even laughed at himself. In spite of all of his misadventures, he became our highly respected pack leader and staunch keeper of the rules and regulations. Reliving his exploits gave hope for the rest of us!

He accomplished so much in his lifetime and even had a book written about his adventures. How awesome is that? Furthermore, having shared some of his escapades this afternoon with you, the reader, made the time pass quickly.

Before moving on to the next image on the Wall of Fame, I leave you with one special photo of Kessen…one that I believe shows his true personality and genuine warmth of spirit. His smiling face says it all. He's our pack leader, our friend as well as the most beloved member of the household…his very own sorority house. Not every dog can be as special as Kessen. I guarantee it…

He's one in a million!

Brighton

As a young puppy, I saw the Wall of Fame during my very first visit to the sorority house, and my eyes were immediately drawn to the photo in the center section of the wall. There, staring back at me front and center, were two incredible poses of the most statuesque dog that I had ever seen. The eyes in each photo seemed to follow me as I moved from one side of the room to the other. Truth be told, that detail was a little bit creepy, and yet, I couldn't take my eyes away from those images. At the time, I asked Kessen about this regal-looking dog. In his own characteristic way, he grinned and began a most interesting tale of the beautiful dog in the photos.

Brighton was her given name, but most everyone called her Brightie. She would one day become my very best friend, but I didn't know this at the time. She was the first female canine to ever cross the threshold of the sorority house, and while her appearance was that of a cuddly and charming puppy, her demeanor was more suggestive of a feral beast.

Jennifer Rae

She was also partly responsible for naming the house the sorority house, but that didn't occur until other females entered the house.

Since I'm new to this storytelling business, I seem to have jumped ahead of myself in the story. So, I'll backtrack a bit and start from the beginning of her captivating reign, and I do mean reign. Brightie came to our household from California when she was just eight weeks old. She was an assistance puppy in training and was the smallest puppy to ever come to the household…weighing in at only ten pounds of flaxen spunk and beauty. Kessen was immediately smitten by her appearance and even had some thoughts of a possible romance down the line as she grew a bit older. However,

She's a cutie!

these thoughts were short-lived when the folks referred to Brightie as his adopted sister. The word *sister* immediately put the brakes on Kessen's plans for future romance. Since Kessen readily adapted to situations, he decided that as Brightie's big brother, his job was to protect her from any forms of danger. Little did he know that Brightie was well prepared to take care of herself, and that he, himself, might be the one needing protection.

From the get-go, Brightie's behavior left a lot to be desired. Sure, puppies were energetic, feisty and fun-loving, but they were rarely enthusiastic biters. Never had Kessen ever come across a puppy whose only goal in life was to challenge and bite anything and everything in sight. She wasn't doing the normal puppy nipping either. Brightie was after blood, and no one got in her way. For the protection of their hands, the folks

even wore leather gloves when they worked with her. They were just as amazed as Kessen was…only Kessen bore the brunt of Brightie's wrath since he didn't have access to leather gloves.

The folks, concerned about Brightie's potential for aggression, talked to

Kessen was her personal pin cushion.

people who knew about her early life in California. The eight weeks after birth has such an impact on a growing puppy, and something had to have happened to her during this time period. As it turned out, Brightie was the first born and smallest puppy in the litter. Often picked on by her siblings due to her petite size, she chose to fight in a *fight or flight* situation. Understandably, she eventually became a bully in an effort to defend herself…possibly the smallest bully ever encountered.

Ultimately, she developed some strong trust issues and came to her new household with a bit of a chip on her shoulder and the need to protect herself at all costs. Her daily routine consisted of charging the adults with her teeth barred and relentlessly biting Kessen at every opportunity. If not for the seriousness of her issues, seeing such a small tyke doing those things might have appeared a bit comical. Nevertheless, as a potential assistance dog, it wasn't acceptable by any stretch of the imagination. While the folks didn't want to send her back to the organization, they knew that her behavior had to change if she were to be trained for assistance. Kessen could not be constantly used as a chew toy for her razor-sharp baby teeth, and she definitely had to stop charging and biting the folks.

In an effort to change her behavior, Brightie was enrolled in a Puppy Kindergarten Class for some additional lessons in socialization with other puppies. The class included six other dogs of various breeds, but the most unusual looking dog was a dog that looked very much like a fox. He was a small, reddish and tan colored puppy with piercing eyes that seemed to dart around the room surveying the surroundings. Brightie had never seen a dog who looked like him before. He was a most unusual breed known as a Shiba Inu. His name was Brutus, which was a bit comical, since his diminutive size denoted much less than brute status. However, from the cautious looks of the other class members, Brightie now had first-hand knowledge of what a real bully looked like.

While she, herself, acted like a bully, she never really knew what she looked like when behaving in that rude manner. Seeing the way Brutus taunted the class members as well as the way he enjoyed their reactions to his behavior made Brightie realize that she definitely had to change her controlling ways. She never wanted other pups to look at her with such apprehension and fear. Of course, Brutus never ever bothered her

No one liked a bully!

because she wasn't intimidated by him. He immediately knew that by the defiant and challenging look in her eyes. Before they had even been introduced, Brutus knew that he had met his match in this elfin-like pup named Brightie.

Brightie became the guardian of the class and because the pups had such great fun together, Brutus felt left out. Not wanting to be alone, he decided to forego his bullying ways, at least for a little while, and became a nicer member of the kindergarten pack. He had to settle for second in command because Brightie became the pack leader for all the right reasons. To be chosen for that respected position meant a lot to Brightie and was her first step toward proper behavior toward others.

The folks, on the other paw, saw how beneficial the class was for her and changed their tactics as well. Since any type of excited voice would set Brightie off into some form of charging or biting, they spoke only in a monotone. All forms of praise were offered in a soft, modulated tone of voice. If corrections were needed, rather than any type of reprimand, they would just leave the room for a few minutes. When they returned, if Brightie behaved herself, the play continued. If not, they would leave the room again. In time, Brightie realized that having them leave her was actually worse than behaving herself. Because of earlier struggles with her littermates, changing her behavior wasn't going to be easy, but she would definitely make the attempt. This determination to change gave her new-found confidence and even led to her calling her foster parents Mom and Dad.

Brightie had a real breakthrough when she was about four months old. Since assistance dogs had to be able to get into all types of carriers, our foster mom was teaching her how to get in and out of an airline crate. Dad was hesitant for our mom to put her face so close to Brightie's mouth, but Mom trusted Brightie and hoped that her trust would be returned. After hesitating a bit, Brightie entered the rather huge acrylic crate, turned herself around and assumed a sitting position at the back wall of the enclosure. She looked so tiny, innocent and incapable of any type of troublesome act. Watching her sitting so calmly, the folks thought that perhaps Brightie was reverting to old behaviors and contemplating her next form of attack, but they wanted to present a relaxed atmosphere for the little tyke. Our mom gave Brightie the release command using a confident yet modulated tone of voice. Low and behold, Brightie came out, curled up on our mom's lap and never bit her again. She was now prepared to trust her family. It was a moment in time that would be long remembered as a special day for Brightie as well as for the rest of the family. To this day, our mom talks about that auspicious moment when she gave presentations about raising potential assistance dogs. It was memorable for all! Kessen especially enjoyed Brightie's behavior adjustment because his days as a pin cushion ended. It truly was a day of celebration for the entire family. Many obstacles remained, but at least it was a good start for all involved.

The next step toward Brightie's socialization was to

work with a special dog named Linus who was also known as The Big Gun. He was quite a dignified and talented Golden Retriever who taught puppy etiquette to ill-behaved puppies.

The Big Gun

Hard to believe that a dog actually did this sort of thing, but Linus helped Kessen when he was just a pup, and he'd do the same for Brightie.

Linus had a very special plan referred to as the Three Step Action Plan. The purpose was to teach pups the correct way to behave with other dogs while in the house and in public. When the puppy did something inappropriate, Step One in Linus' plan was to issue a curled lip with a bit of a quiver to the offending puppy. If that didn't alert the pup to misbehavior, Linus would then go to Step Two which was to add a low-toned growl to the process. Seeing that curled, quivering lip and hearing that eerie growl usually did the trick. However, when those two steps didn't work as in Brightie's case, Linus advanced to Step Three. With the speed of light, a quick but efficient muffled snap was issued...barely missing the misbehaving pooch. The combination of those three steps was always met with success. Soon Brightie realized that she had met her match in Linus and recognized his elite status. In addition to these unique methods, Brightie would learn to respect Kessen as the pack leader in the household. With only two dogs in the pack, Linus would teach Brightie that Kessen was still the leader, and as such, was to be respected. Linus faced some challenges, but he was going to spend a week with both Kessen and Brightie, and he was prepared for anything...even Brightie. After a few days with Linus and his repeated use of the Three Step Action Plan, Brightie totally understood her unique position in the canine pack, readily learned appropriate dog to dog interaction as well as control of her biting. Brightie made big advances in terms of her behaviors.

Good Friends

After all of the initial turmoil involved with Linus' arrival, Brightie and Linus actually became friends. They met at various times, and Linus took her aside and shared words of wisdom regarding appropriate puppy behavior. Knowing that Linus did the very same things with Kessen made Brightie's moments with Linus very special. Through all of the training, Brightie realized that Kessen was not only her big brother but also her very own hero. Linus left after his week with Kessen and Brightie, and both dogs were really pleased with the results. Kessen was released from his role as an in-house pin cushion, and Brightie had the tools to become a better puppy in training. Everything was well with the world…so far.

But, Brightie still had a lot to learn. Kessen taught her about the necessity of sharing…especially food and toys. The first lessons didn't go very well since Brightie was accustomed to having her way, but eventually she came around to Kessen's teachings. She faced all sorts of challenges like not eating mulch from the dog run, not running after butterflies and above all, not jumping on a hornet nestled in a plant in the yard. This last bit of knowledge took a bit of painful re-learning on her part plus a small dose of antihistamines from our mom, but overall, Kessen didn't think that Brightie was afraid of anything…that is, until she faced the basement stairs

Living in a ranch style house left few opportunities for going up and down stairs, but once in a while, going down to the basement was a requirement. So, Kessen took it upon himself to acquaint Brightie with the proper way to go down and up the stairs. An assistance dog doesn't run down the stairs but waits for the command to walk down one step at a time. This procedure is essential, and Kessen wanted to impart the importance of following the process. Off they went to the utility room and faced the open door that led to the basement.

Fortunately, the door was open, and they had easy access to the stairs leading down to the basement. Brightie had a smug look on her face as they approached the doorway as if to say that she wasn't afraid of anything. The challenge of going up and down stairs would prove Brightie's courage to Kessen. She was licking her chops in anticipation as she boldly approached the

Not happening today!

stairs…grinning from ear to ear at the potential of showing Kessen how brave she really was. But, suddenly her courage was short-lived because of what she did next…Brightie looked down! Once she saw the depth of those stairs, she knew that not only was she not going to go down them but, she wasn't coming back up either.

Nevertheless, Brightie, having to maintain her image of being fearless, wasn't about to let Kessen see her fear of the stairs. Instead, she assumed a casual pose at the top of the stairs and yawned loudly a few times as if to demonstrate her boredom with the exercise. Kessen, being the wise pack leader, knew that yawning was sometimes a sign of potential stress in dogs but did not mention this possibility to Brightie.

He expected this nonchalance from her since most of Brightie's bravado was her way of protecting herself from showing fear and being hurt by others. Showing strength, in spite of being inwardly fearful, saved her from the type of hurt she experienced from her siblings as a very young pup. Kessen understood her mindset and didn't acknowledge her fears. Instead, he was determined to help her with her stair issue. So, he demonstrated how to go down the stairs…taking each step slowly and one step at a time. When he reached the bottom, he encouraged her to follow his example and meet him at the bottom.

At first, she was reluctant to even look at Kessen at the bottom of the stairs, so he came back up and tried again. This time, they would go down the stairs together. Taking one step at a time, Kessen began his descent, but unfortunately, Brightie didn't follow his lead. Since going up and down stairs was an important task in a dog's life, Kessen wasn't about to give up on her. Once again, Kessen went up to encourage her and, to his complete surprise, discovered that she was nowhere to be found. She had left the area entirely and had gone into another room. He found her lounging with a squeak toy as if that stair incident never happened.

Kessen, being a clever pack leader, knew better than to say anything about the stair lesson. He knew that after a while, Brightie would attempt it again and be successful. He also knew that when she did attempt the stairs again, she would do it on her own just to prove to herself that she could. Brightie had that sort of spunk, and Kessen admired her for it. About a week later, Kessen heard her running up and down the stairs. He said nothing about it to her…he just grinned at his insights into her behavior.

During the following weeks, Brightie continued with her training as a potential assistance dog. She learned her required commands quickly and often joined Kessen for play time following her training classes. In spite of their jaw sparring and air snapping, they were now very compatible and rarely got into disagreements. Even though they each had their own dog beds, Brightie often enjoyed sleeping with Kessen. While she took up most of the bed, Kessen tolerated it because she was, of course, his little sister, and she boasted that he was her hero. For a little tyke, she sure knew how to get her way.

In spite of her changes in behavior, Brightie still had a stubborn streak that usually reared its ugly head when she didn't get her way. It wasn't a very pretty sight when this occurred. Because of her petite stature and innocent facial features, Brightie was often mistaken for a much younger pup and used this fact to her

Brightie knew how to get her way.

advantage whenever convenient. Misbehaviors were often overlooked, tolerated or justified as follies of a youthful puppy. She had the *special look* and definitely knew how to work the room.

In addition to Brightie using her endearing appearance to her advantage, one of her favorite methods for getting her way was to throw a full-blown tantrum. She'd roll over on her back, kick up her legs and shriek as loudly as she could. Her intensified screeching resonated through the air as if blasted from an amplified megaphone. Depending upon the reaction of onlookers, the duration of the tantrum lasted as long as it took to get her way. Brightie was petite but definitely not short on endurance. The longer she screeched, the louder she became.

Her opportunities for tantrums were varied as well as numerous. If Kessen wouldn't give up one of his toys to her, she assumed the tantrum position and commenced shrieking. Sometimes, Kessen would give in and let her have it just so she'd stop the infernal screeching. He realized that giving in to her shenanigans only encouraged future tantrums, but his hearing was at stake. Most of the time, Kessen would just walk away and take his toy with him. He knew that if he went to the other end of the house during her outburst, she'd be so busy howling that she wouldn't even notice. It was a win-win situation for Kessen since he still had his toy, and his hearing was no longer at risk. She wasn't the only one who had ideas that worked.

Brightie knew that she had the best advantage for getting her way when she was out in public with the folks. Wearing her cape and representing her organization was special, and the folks wanted and expected her best behavior. However, wanting good behavior and getting good behavior were two different things, and the folks didn't always get it. One day in particular, our mom was buying some books from the neighborhood bookstore where everyone knew and admired Brightie. It happened to be a sale day at the store, and numerous people filled the aisles. Purchases were going slowly, and Brightie was getting bored just standing in the check-out line with our mom. Since she was missing her play time by being in that line, Brightie decided to work her magic…the infamous tantrum. She proceeded to throw the tantrum of all tantrums. To top it off, she'd have a huge audience since customers filled the store for the book sales. Brightie was certain that our mom would rush her out of the store once she began her screeching. In a slow and most dramatic way, Brightie assumed the tantrum position. Our mom, seeing Brightie slowly roll onto her back, knew what was coming but didn't make any move to stop her. This momentarily confused Brightie since she was deliberately giving our mom a warning of what was going to happen. In her mind, Brightie believed that by issuing a warning, she gave our mom the opportunity to whisk her out of the store before the first full breath of screeching commenced.

Thinking that our mom was bluffing by not leaving the store, Brightie took some deep breaths, filled her lungs to capacity and began screeching. As Brightie kicked up her legs and shrieked at the top of her lungs, all eyes turned to the disturbance, and a bit of a crowd formed around Brightie. Not knowing what else might happen, the onlookers stayed a safe enough distance away so as not to become part of the drama. Out of the corner of her eye, Brightie glanced at our mom and noticed that our mom wasn't even looking at her. Instead, our mom was looking at greeting cards and paying no attention to her at all. So, Brightie shrieked even louder, but that didn't work either.

The realization that our mom wasn't going to give in to her foolish attempt to get her way was shocking to Brightie. She was losing her powers to control others, and her continuous shrieking was making her dizzy. As if that weren't bad enough, a woman, who had been witnessing the dramatic event, smiled at our mom and mentioned that she had a grandchild who did the same thing. Both women laughed, and Brightie was not only disappointed but really exhausted from her unsuccessful exhibition. Her tantrum ended without the desired result, and the wait resumed in the check-out line as if nothing had happened. Though Brightie realized that she had lost some of her power with the adults while in public, she still had considerable control over Kessen. For now, that would have to be enough for her.

The weeks turned into months as Brightie continued her training and was getting much better in public. Her tantrums occurred less frequently, and thankfully, never happened when the folks took her to church. The outcome might have been quite different if Brightie had chosen that particular venue for her dramatic episodes. She liked to get her way, but she wasn't totally insensitive to others' feelings. A tantrum in church would have been offensive and far beneath Brightie's image of herself. She considered herself to be a delightful diva and prided herself in that description. After all, she did have limits to her capacity to create chaos.

Sometimes, the backyard became a training area as

opposed to a play yard for Brightie. Our mom would get her dressed in her working gear and off they'd go into the yard for reviewing her commands. Brightie really enjoyed the refreshing atmosphere of the yard, and thought it was such a magical place. There were so many flowers, shrubs, bushes and trees

Her yard was magical.   surrounding the area, and all were in full bloom. Maintaining a perfect Sit/Stay in the midst of such splendor gave her an opportunity to appreciate the wonderful life that she shared with her family. These moments were both happy and calming for Brightie.

Aside from her diva-like moments, Brightie also had quite a playful side. When she wasn't wearing her cape, she knew that the yard became her playground, and her imagination soared. She would often zigzag her way around the bushes at full speed, hunt for imaginary foes, chase butterflies, and sometimes take a bite or two of a day lily as she ran by. The yard was full of surprises, and the only boundary was her imagination. When our mom and dad would come out to the yard to get her, Brightie would hide in plain sight using the concrete statue as her shield. This was by far her all-time favorite hiding place. Even though

She loved to hide.

our mom and dad saw Brightie with her head resting on the statue, they pretended not to see her and made a big deal about not being able to find her. Eventually, Brightie jumped out from her hiding place, ran around the yard and surprised her folks. Her yard was truly a happy place for her, and she'd miss those cherished moments when her time with the family came to an end.

In two weeks, she would be saying good bye to the family and going off to advanced training. In appreciation for Brightie's spending time with them at the sorority house, the folks took her for the traditional Canine Fun Swim at the hydrotherapy center. They were most anxious to see if Brightie enjoyed the water-world experience as much as Kessen did. When they entered the pool house, Brightie took one look at that huge pool, and her inner-diva emerged. She immediately braced her legs on the concrete walkway and refused to move. There was no way that she was getting near that expanse of water. The folks tried tempting her with dried liver morsels, but even her favorite treats weren't enough to get Brightie anywhere near the ramp…let alone into the pool. Because they didn't want to force Brightie to do something that she apparently wasn't comfortable doing, the folks gathered their things, and the three of them left the pool house.

While our folks were somewhat disappointed that Brightie didn't share the same enthusiasm for swimming as Kessen, they weren't entirely surprised by her behavior. Even on a good day, Brightie didn't like to get the pads of her paws wet. She was quite finicky about that and even refused going outside if there were even a hint of moisture in the air or early morning dew on the deck leading to the dog run. Even though she had her quirks, the folks still loved her to bits and would miss her dearly when she left to further her education.

Brightie went off to advanced training but never really had the same desire for service as Kessen did. On one paw, she preferred having things done for her instead of her doing things for others. In her mind, service meant *room service*. She never thought of it as being selfish…just being honest. After all, not all dogs wanted to be service dogs. Brightie, being a self-professed diva, preferred a different lifestyle.

On the other paw, she really liked the training sessions, enjoyed representing the organization at fund raisers, thought she looked spectacular in her cape and had fun meeting new people and other dogs. Every experience in public was exciting, but she just didn't know if assistance work was right for her. She knew how important service was to Kessen, and a part of her wished that she felt the same way. But as frivolous as she was, Brightie was realistic about her goals in life. She looked forward to the advanced training experience and truly wanted to give it a chance in spite of these feelings. Perhaps the experience might change her attitude as well as her future goals. Life held many adventures, and anything was possible.

Brightie remained in advanced training for almost three months before the folks got the dreaded phone call…the one that all foster puppy raisers feared. Brightie was being released from the program. While she trained well and knew all of her commands, the trainers recognized that she just didn't seem enthusiastic about working toward assistance. In her defense, Brightie gave it a good try, and that was all that mattered.

Following that dreaded phone call about Brightie's release, the folks immediately drove out to the training facility to adopt her as a permanent member of their family. Kessen, being part of the welcoming committee, accompanied them on the trip. But, when they pulled into the driveway of the facility, Kessen had a complete meltdown. Panting heavily and whining loudly, he recalled the unfortunate time he spent there and momentarily lost his grip on reality. Upon seeing Kessen so overwhelmed, the folks attempted to comfort him by speaking in low, soothing tones while lightly massaging his body. Those gentle actions seemed to reassure him. Once Kessen realized that he wasn't going back, he eventually calmed down. After witnessing Kessen's extreme response to returning to the center, the folks were really concerned about Brightie's state of mind and physical condition since she had been there for over three months. Kessen wasn't there nearly that long and was devastated by the experience. Would Brightie be that overwhelmed as well?

Mom quickly entered the facility to complete the necessary paperwork for the formal adoption and was anxious to see Brightie. Dad stayed in the car with Kessen and hoped for the best. Tension was high while waiting for them to come out, but relief filled their senses as they saw Brightie leaving the building. Out she walked as if she had been staying at a Doggie Day Spa. It was apparent that absolutely nothing bothered that dog. Seeing her looking so healthy and perky lifted everyone's spirits. She hopped into the back seat of the car with Kessen as if she had never left them, and off they went…a happy family.

After a week of relaxation, Brightie was told that she would be trained for animal-assisted therapy. She had forgotten that every dog, who lived in the sorority house, had to have a job. Since she already knew most of the commands, her training went well, and she soon completed the new training program. Now, all she and our mom had to do was wait for the right program for the two of them.

Brightie's work schedule filled up very quickly, and, surprisingly, she didn't mind at all. She really enjoyed this type of service, so being a therapy dog was the perfect fit for her. Brightie eagerly volunteered at the nearby hospital by spending time in the children's waiting room. They played games with her, put stickers all over her

Off to Work!

body and even took her for short walks in the hospital's hallway. They loved having her visit, and Brightie enjoyed it as well.

Brightie also volunteered at the county's detention center twice a month and worked with boys living there. She and five other dogs participated in a program that helped the boys learn about caring for and training dogs. The crew included two Huskies, two Collies, Brightie and one other Labrador Retriever. The boys would select a dog and work on teaching commands and brushing them while sharing information about the dogs they had at home.

They worked on an activity called Rally Obedience or Rally-O. This activity involved a designated course that contained numbered stations, and each station had a sign that contained one, two or three commands. The handler and the dog worked as a team and scored points for each station's commands done correctly. As the exercise progressed, the commands, as well as the course itself, became more difficult. It was a challenging, fun-filled activity because the course was never the same, and the commands were changed each time the dogs came to the detention facility. Brightie really enjoyed this experience, but occasionally something would happen that changed the enjoyment of the activity.

During this one specific session, all of the dogs were working well with their handlers on the Rally-O course. Everything was going well until a section of folding chairs at the far end of the room suddenly came crashing to the floor. The noise reverberated loudly and startled all of the dogs. Brightie, who was working with her partner closest to the origin of the noise, slipped on the shiny floor and injured her hip. While she momentarily limped a bit, she was more frightened than injured. However, from that episode alone, she developed a fear shiny floors. Long-term problems often occur when a dog is hurt or frightened in some way. Unfortunately, this incident and the resulting fear hampered Brightie's ability to go to various places for volunteering.

The folks weren't sure how to help her get past this fear of shiny floors but relied on Kessen for his leadership assistance. Since both dogs volunteered at the hospital and the hospital had a multitude of shiny floors, it was important for Brightie to overcome her fears. So, Kessen became her source of courage in canine form to help with her issues.

Mom and Dad took the two dogs to the hospital on a day when they weren't scheduled to volunteer. Together, they practiced just having Brightie follow Kessen through the entrance doors. They did this over and over again until Brightie walked through the front doors in a relaxed manner. The next day, Kessen led her through the entrance doors and into the vestibule. Again, this exercise was done under Kessen's guidance and Brightie's total reliance on him for courage. Gradually, she was able to get to her destination at the far end of the huge hospital with Kessen walking behind her rather than in front of her. Even though it took almost three weeks to accomplish, Brightie had regained her courage due to his leadership. The folks were so grateful for

Kessen was her hero.

Kessen's part in Brightie's overcoming her fear of the shiny floors and would always remember what he had done for her. Kessen really understood what helping others was all about...especially since it involved helping his best friend through a difficult time in her life.

Brightie and Kessen were also in the reading program at the library together. While Kessen was at his best in this program, she sometimes needed encouragement. She was not what you might call a *morning dog*. In fact, she rarely reached her perky state before noon, so this reading program was a bit of a challenge for her. To prevent Brightie from falling asleep while a child was reading to her, our mom would position the tip of her shoe under her stomach. If Brightie started closing her eyes, our mom would just raise the tip of her shoe, and that slight movement returned Brightie to an attentive listening mode.

In spite of her occasional lapse into momentary dreamland, Brightie really enjoyed meeting with the children in the reading program. However, on one particular day, her sleeping habits drastically changed. While she was waiting for

Rufus was a real hunk!

the children to arrive, she caught sight of the most handsome Parson Jack Russell Terrier that she had ever seen. As he surveyed the room, he had a twinkle in his eyes that spelled trouble, and Brightie knew immediately who he was. His name was Rufus, and his reputation as quite the Casanova among the canines

preceded him. He was known for his debonair style, quick wit and charming demeanor. Rumor had it that he could melt ice with just his smile, and Brightie didn't doubt that one bit since he sure was a handsome dude.

When their eyes met as he glanced across the room, she was immediately smitten. Brightie knew right then and there that she'd never fall asleep again in the program while Rufus was there. As he looked at her, the intensity in his eyes signaled that he felt the same way. They had to meet...they just had to.

Kessen didn't get it. He was very protective of his
adopted sister and knew all about Rufus
and his philandering. While it sounded
like Kessen was a bit jealous of Rufus'
reputation with the canines of female
persuasion, he just wanted to protect
Brightie from getting hurt. Sure, Rufus
had it all…he was smart, charming and
had an uncanny way with the females
that made them swoon over him. Kessen

Rufus had it all!

just wanted to make sure that Rufus wasn't going to take
advantage of Brightie's first encounter with exciting puppy
love. She was unskilled in that area and consequently, fell for
him…and fell hard.

Rufus was all that she talked about on the way home
from the reading program. Kessen knew that if he told her all
that he knew about Rufus, she would resent his intrusion into
her life. So, he kept silent and just hoped that reason might
overcome her fascination with this dog…a dog one might
typically see on the cover of Handsome Dog Quarterly
Magazine. A sensible pup left the house this morning for the

library reading program and came home
dreaming of a future with a dog that she hadn't
even met. Brightie needed to take a trip on the
reality train and fast. That night, all she could
dream about was Rufus…the twinkle in his
eyes and smiles from across the room. She was

Her Destiny

positive that he definitely liked her.

She spent her days thinking about him, picturing his
face and hoping to meet him at the next reading program
assignment. He was most certainly the dog of her dreams and

her destiny. As it turned out, Brightie didn't have long to wait for fate to intervene. She, Kessen and the folks were scheduled to volunteer at a book store gift-wrapping session during the holidays. Donations would go toward the organization, and Brightie and Kessen were always anxious to participate. People were constantly greeting and petting them while waiting for their gifts to be wrapped, so it was a fun gig. Brightie usually did these types of functions with Kessen and was happy for the canine companionship. She did, however, hope that Rufus might just show up to assist with the fund raiser, but that was just wishful thinking on her part.

Brightie's star-struck eyes almost crossed when she saw her one and only true love enter the store. There, in all his

They were the perfect couple.

canine splendor, was Rufus and his partner. They exchanged pleasantries as dogs do in their own peculiar manner, and both seemed quite happy with each other's company. This relationship was a dream come true for Brightie, and truth be told, Rufus seemed to be quite enamored with Brightie. Kessen, noticing the attention Rufus gave to Brightie, thought that perhaps his assumptions about Rufus were incorrect. Maybe Rufus really cared for Brightie and wasn't just toying with her feelings. Kessen finally accepted that Rufus' intentions were honorable and didn't pressure Brightie about her feelings for Rufus anymore.

While Brightie considered them to be a couple, Rufus never quite committed to that relationship. He was a free spirit and boasted of liking the lady dogs...all shapes and sizes. Even though Brightie experienced a slight hint of apprehension when he spoke like this, she just thought that he was teasing her. In spite of her concern, Brightie was optimistic and felt that their devotion to each other would withstand the test of time. Kessen couldn't believe that Brightie, the daring and fearless pup, talked in such a manner. Love must really be blind because Brightie was seriously in need of a guide dog.

However, their relationship hit a bump in the road at a fund raising dog-walk a few weeks later. All sorts of breeds were represented, and colorful booths lined the walkway that would be the path for the dogs and their handlers. Kessen, Brightie and Rufus represented their therapy organization at the dog-walk when the inevitable happened. A graceful, petite, tan and white Cavalier King Charles Spaniel sauntered past the booth. When she saw Rufus, she flaunted her femininity by waving her feathered tail in a most provocative manner. Rufus was not only captivated but also instantly smitten with the diminutive debutante. Brightie was tossed aside by a miniature version of something that, in her mind, only resembled a real dog. Needless to say, she was heartbroken at being dumped by Rufus. Her first venture into the realm of love turned ugly in an instant. Kessen tried to console her, but she just wanted to be left alone.

When their session at the donation booth ended, Brightie, Kessen and the folks didn't stay around for the festivities. Not a word was shared between Brightie and Rufus since the brazen arrival of the Cavalier King Charles Spaniel. Brightie had to face the facts that their relationship was over. However, Kessen, being the big brother, wanted to take Rufus behind the booth and give him a piece of his mind. Brightie, regaining her sense of humor, told Kessen that he really couldn't afford to give away any part his mind...not even a small part of it for a good cause. They both laughed at that

Her First Love

prospect, and Kessen immediately knew that she was going to be fine.

After a very quiet ride home, Brightie spent most of the afternoon by herself. Though her feelings were hurt, Brightie knew that while Rufus was a wonderful dog, he was what he claimed to be...a free spirit. That's what made him so very attractive to the canines of the female persuasion. However, the next time that she fell in love, she'd be a bit more careful with her choice of suitors.

Although she didn't show it at the time, Brightie was most grateful for Kessen's good advice during her first attempt in the kennel of love. He was a wonderful big brother to her and always watched out for her welfare. They made a pretty good team not only in the assisted therapy gigs but in the brother-sister relationship as well.

Brightie started thinking about taking that relationship to a different level…an in-house, working relationship. Since the folks were foster puppy raisers for potential assistance dogs, each year they brought a puppy into the house for the first twelve months of his or her training. Now that both Kessen and Brightie were permanent members of the family, they served as mentors for each new puppy and taught them what dogs teach each other well: bite inhibition, appropriate dog to dog interaction and pack behavior. That was unquestionably a job that they did well.

Brightie's mind was whirling at full speed with the possibility of formulating an official title for their new endeavor. Together, they would be co-captains of the Socialization Squad and ultimately share all of the responsibilities with each new pup that came to their sorority house for training. Kessen loved the concept as well as the official squad's title but not the singular idea of sharing in the puppy's training responsibilities.

They were equal partners.

He thought of himself as being in a supervisory capacity, but he was a reasonable canine and agreed to the shared duties. On that particular day, the Socialization Squad became a reality. Now, they were equal partners in this new and exciting endeavor.

Brightie and Kessen enjoyed a number of escapades in the years to come. As Brightie fell in and out of love, Kessen, her big brother and hero, was there to pick up the pieces. They shared many more escapades together, and I look forward to the possibility of sharing these new adventures with you, the reader, in the near future...

Brightie was the resident diva!

Marnie

The fourth canine to cross the threshold of the sorority house was none other than sweet and petite Marnie. As her image stared back at me from the Wall of Fame, it was clear that the photographer captured her spirit, elegance and self-confidence in that one definitive pose. While Kessen shared some of her escapades with me, he admitted that she was, in fact, one of his favorite puppies. His partiality wasn't because she was the calmest of pups, but because she demonstrated genuine sincerity and kindness toward others on a daily basis. These qualities were his measure of favoritism. However, I must stop myself again because I jumped ahead in the telling of Marnie's story. Storytelling isn't as easy as it sounds, and in order to be accurate, I need to go back to her beginning... Marnie's arrival.

During the days prior to Marnie's arrival, Kessen and Brightie recognized the signs of a new puppy on the way to the sorority house. Small crates appeared in various rooms of the house, and gates were positioned across various hallways. An area of the kitchen was transformed into a puppy play area complete with a small crate and food bowls. These were all very clear signs of puppy preparation, and both Kessen and Brightie were filled with excitement over the puppy's impending arrival.

They were most anxious to meet this new puppy because she was the first puppy being mentored by the Socialization Squad. Teaching her acceptable canine behavior was an enormous responsibility, but the Squad was ready to handle any behavioral issue that came their way. First and foremost, Kessen and Brightie had to get to know this petite newcomer who would alter their world for the next fifteen months.

They knew very little about her other than what was mentioned by their folks during the week. According to what they heard, this pup was a female, black Labrador Retriever and was very small for her age. That wasn't much information for Kessen and Brightie to go on, but any time a puppy entered the house, excitement was guaranteed.

Waiting for the folks to return from the training facility with the new puppy seemed to take forever. Kessen thought the extreme weather had something to do with their delay. The heavy snowfall the night before caused treacherous conditions on the highways and streets. According to the news, some roads were even impassable. This information caused some safety concerns, but our dad was a good driver and would be very careful on the dangerous snow-filled roads.

Finally, they heard the garage door creaking open and the ice crackling under the tires of the car as Mom and Dad's car pulled into the driveway. Their hackles bristled with excitement over meeting the new puppy. As they watched the door knob slowly turn, their hackles zoomed up and down their backs with anticipation. When the door finally opened, a tiny, somewhat timid pup stared up at them with huge, captivating eyes that completely dominated her face. Kessen and Brightie immediately felt an emotional connection as well as a need to protect this little puppy. It was obvious that she wasn't quite sure what to do when faced with one giant dog and another mini-giant looking inquisitively at her, but she gathered her courage, took a deep breath and tentatively walked into the kitchen area.

Kessen and Brightie followed her slowly so as not to frighten the little newcomer. She seemed quite polite in that her first endeavor was to sniff each of them appropriately. Even at her early age, she knew enough to recognize the pack leader and went directly to Kessen, but Brightie believed that she just

She was enchanting!

chose the giant dog first because of his size. Once the greetings ended, it was time to get a good look at this elfin puppy who would probably be spending the next fifteen months under their care. Upon first glance, the dogs were immediately drawn to the penetrating eyes that seemed to fully dominate her small face. In addition to having the distinctive, roly-poly puppy build, Marnie's shiny ebony coat had a wild, fluffy appearance that was endearing to humans. The velvety texture of her ears was in direct contrast to her coat, and that variation in textures made her sparkling eyes seem even more noticeable. She was definitely all puppy from the top of her coal-black nose to the tip of her tail. Between Marnie's polite demeanor and her striking

Marnie was a winner!

appearance, Kessen and Brightie were convinced that this puppy was destined for success in the sorority house and could be a major accomplishment for the Socialization Squad. Once again, they had a win-win situation on their paws.

The days following Marnie's arrival went very smoothly for both the folks and the dogs. Marnie was easily house trained and slept with no howling. Even being taken out in the middle of the night was fun for her. She especially enjoyed the snow…the deeper the better. Since she was very small, our dad would go out in the blustering cold weather and shovel an area of the dog run just for her. When Marnie was let out into the dog run, rather than go to the shoveled area, she'd dive into the section that had the most snow. Day or night, that little tyke headed for the deepest part of the snow. Sometimes, the folks only caught a glimpse of her head peeking out of the snow, but Marnie loved it.

Because of her amazing eyes, the folks affectionately gave her the quirky nickname of Marnie Google. They claimed that she had the Goo-Goo-Googliest Eyes. None of the dogs even knew what that meant, but in all honesty, a number of things that the folks said never made much sense either. So, the dogs just went along with Marnie's new nickname.

Most dogs were fascinated by balls and squeak toys... but not Marnie. She was totally captivated by daily housework. Give her an open cabinet door at floor level, and she'd organize the cabinet by taking things out and then putting the items back. While they may

Housekeeper's Helper

not be returned to the shelves in the correct order, they were, nevertheless, returned to the cabinet. When our mom folded

Laundry was her specialty!

the laundry, Marnie rushed to the opened door of the dryer, quickly pulled the clothes out and dropped them on the floor. Finding the fabric softener sheet inside the dryer was like finding a tasty bone filled with juicy marrow. She was momentarily ecstatic but would then shred that sheet to pieces. Laundry day was such an exciting time of the week for her.

Moving throw rugs around was Marnie's specialty. She often dragged a rug from one room to another, and then hauled it back a little later in the day. Kessen believed that if she had hands instead of paws, she'd be moving furniture all over the house. Marnie even placed her toys in a laundry basket and then used the basket as her bed. If nothing else, this young pup was an efficiency expert and definitely enjoyed doing housework. Marnie was destined for a career in service... cleaning service!

Kessen and Brightie didn't escape Marnie's working mode either. When Kessen left his toys on the floor, Marnie rushed in and took them to her laundry basket. She collected his toys when he wasn't around out of respect for his position as pack leader. If he slept with a toy next to him or clutched one in his paws, she didn't dare touch it. After all, she thought of herself as being a well-mannered puppy, and taking his toy while he slept would be considered very rude behavior.

Brightie, on the other paw, wasn't given the same courtesy as Kessen. Marnie would pull a toy right out of Brightie's mouth, rush back to her laundry basket, drop the toy in and then climb on top of all of the toys for a cushioned nap. Marnie also knew that Brightie would make no attempt to retrieve her toy because she was reluctant to reach into the laundry

Marnie took comfortable naps!

basket...even to retrieve a stolen toy. Retrieving objects would take some effort, and anything that involved effort was never in Brightie's daily itinerary. Brightie really didn't mind Marnie's silliness at all. In fact, Brightie rather enjoyed watching Marnie clean up toys since her obsession with housework was comparable to having a live-in cleaning service. Without even lifting a paw, Brightie's toys were put away. It was a win-win situation for everybody.

Marnie also had a toy bag that was given to her by a neighbor. Both Kessen and Brightie rolled their eyes when they

saw another potential hiding place for their toys. Marnie was in her glory...another handy storage place. She'd only put her special toys in that toy bag and often checked the inside of the bag to make sure that neither Kessen nor Brightie

Handy Storage

took any toys out. She really had nothing to worry about since Kessen believed it was beneath the dignity of his position to be reaching into a toy bag, and Brightie was fearful of putting her head into anything that might mess up her appearance. Once again, Marnie selected a safe place for her treasures and proved that she was one crafty canine.

As she grew older, Marnie's assault on housework continued. She was a rather small puppy when she first came to the sorority house and, even at five or six months of age, was still a bit of a munchkin. Because she wasn't tall enough to reach the kitchen counters, she often put her front paws on either Brightie or Kessen's backs in order to see what was on the counters or to see over the gate. Kessen and Brightie tolerated her behavior because aside

Brightie was her step stool!

from the housework obsession, she was a considerate and loving dog.

While she played appropriately with Kessen, Brightie and neighbor's dogs, Marnie seemed to prefer the company of people more than dogs. She was always excited to meet new people and was most at ease with our mom. According to Kessen, Marnie followed Mom around most of the day...that was, of course, when Marnie wasn't picking up toys, moving throw rugs or checking the dryer for fabric softener sheets. She sat by our mom's side while dinner was being made and quietly positioned herself under the table while the folks ate their meals. When the folks watched television in the evening, Marnie curled up by our mom's favorite recliner until it was time to go to bed, or sometimes she just fell asleep under the end table by our mom's side. Not even Brightie could entice Marnie into after-dinner play when our mom was around. Though Kessen and Brightie thought it a bit unusual, at least their toys were safe from Marnie's grasp when Mom was in the room.

Marnie wasn't a total goodie-four-paws and was a bit of a mischief maker when she wasn't doing housework. Kessen and Brightie always knew when she was up to something because her eyes would sparkle a bit more than usual. Every evening, our mom read the newspaper while sitting in her favorite recliner. Since being on the furniture was forbidden for all canines except Kessen, Marnie would often attempt to climb into our mom's lap while she was reading. She didn't dare jump into our mom's lap like most dogs wanting to cuddle. Instead, she eased into it by slowly moving her body up the side of the recliner. If Mom stopped reading the newspaper and looked down at her, Marnie would instantly stop what she was doing and look away. Once Mom resumed reading, Marnie would again continue creeping her way up the side of the lounger. Now, Mom knew exactly what she was attempting to do but enjoyed watching Marnie's attempt at fooling her. Eventually, Mom would allow Marnie to creep all the way up into her lap and then acted totally surprised to see her there. They both loved that game and played it often.

One day in particular, Marnie did the unspeakable and climbed onto the recliner while our folks were in another room. She just wanted to see what it felt like to sit in a chair like a person. Marnie loved the unobstructed view from the seat of the recliner and settled comfortably against a decorative throw

She had to hide!

pillow that hugged the corner of the recliner. Suddenly, she heard the folks walking through the hall and didn't quite know what to do. Since she didn't have time to jump off of the recliner without being seen, she decided to hide behind the throw pillow in the corner of the chair. It really wasn't a well thought out plan since Marnie was considerably larger than the pillow. As the folks walked through the hall, they immediately spotted Marnie making that futile attempt to hide behind the pillow. While trying not to laugh at the situation, they questioned where Marnie might be. Upon hearing that, Marnie burrowed her head deeper behind the pillow. Seeing this forty pound, black Labrador Retriever hiding behind a tiny throw pillow was a hilarious sight, yet the folks didn't want to encourage Marnie's behavior by giving her any kind of attention. The folks suppressed their laughter while they walked past the recliner, but immediately laughed out loud when they entered the other room. Once they were totally out of sight, Marnie immediately jumped off the recliner and ran to where Kessen and Brightie were sitting on the other side of the room. Even though she expected the *stink-eye* and customary lecture from Kessen, Marnie was as pleased as a pooch stealing a dropped cookie from the floor at her successful attempt at fooling the folks.

Kessen and Brightie had watched the entire scenario from across the room and could not believe that the folks pretended not to see Marnie on the recliner. They'd have to be blind to miss her rather large body sticking out from behind the small pillow. From past experience, both Kessen and Brightie knew that the folks definitely weren't blind but also had "eyes in the backs of their heads." They saw

Marnie expected the stink-eye!

everything that went on in the house and rarely ignored any form of misbehavior. Maybe seeing Marnie's mischievous side pleased them since it was so contrary to her typical prim and proper behavior. That had to be the main reason for not reprimanding her. People's reactions were often so very confusing and inconsistent. These human tendencies make it very difficult for dogs to anticipate their actions.

Kessen chose not to give Marnie his customary look of disappointment, a.k.a. the *stink-eye,* nor did he lecture her regarding the recliner caper. On that day, her actions proved that she was so much more than just a house-cleaning, people-loving enthusiast. She was, in fact, living up to her heritage and becoming a true, fun-loving Labrador Retriever. In Kessens's mind, it was a proud day for the Labrador Retrievers of the world.

In the weeks that followed, Marnie regularly attended obedience classes just as all of the dogs did while in training. She loved the classes and made numerous friends. Her favorite playmate was a tiny, blonde Pomeranian pup named Hercules. It was an impressive name for such a diminutive puppy, but the name referred to his attitude rather than his size. He believed and acted as if he were actually a big dog in a small body. Watching his bold actions toward much larger dogs was hilarious and sometimes even intimidating to the larger dogs. Perhaps they didn't retaliate because of Hercules' size. After all, getting even might identify them as bullies, and not one canine wanted that demeaning label at this level of obedience classes.

As the classes progressed, Hercules and Marnie were often paired together for various exercises...especially for practicing controlled greetings. In terms of size, they were a comical-looking team but worked extremely well together. Hercules had to take quite a few more steps than Marnie when walking by her side, but Marnie deliberately walked a bit slower to accommodate Hercules' accelerated steps. They shared two six-week sessions of obedience classes together, but since Hercules had learned enough in those classes to be a well-behaved pet, his owner decided not to enroll him in any further classes. Marnie missed him in the next few classes, but she also made a number of new friends in future classes.

Marnie enjoyed learning and progressed quickly in the obedience classes. She was offered the opportunity to enter the advanced class even though the other class members were much older dogs. If anything, Marnie embraced the spirit of adventure and enjoyed trying new things…even if they were a bit intimidating. When the other class members saw this munchkin of a dog entering their territory, they were at first extremely apprehensive. After all, they were members of the elite advanced class and didn't want their sessions changed in any way to accommodate a younger dog. However, after seeing how poised, confident and technically skilled Marnie was, they enthusiastically welcomed her into the group. She grasped the new routines quickly, enjoyed the camaraderie shared by the older dogs, and in the final advanced class competition, she even won a medal for the youngest puppy to receive such a high score. It was a proud day for trainers, dogs and owners alike.

Since Marnie was well-behaved in all situations, our folks increased her public outings. She regularly attended church services on Sundays and especially enjoyed the music and the singing. On one particular Sunday, the pastor had invited a group of violinists to perform during the service. Marnie had never heard the sound of violins before and was initially taken aback by the reverberation in her ears as the musicians played. She gradually got used to it and actually found it to be quite relaxing. However, not all of the congregation's voices adapted well to the sounds of the violins.

While our mom and dad always sang along to the music as best they could, not all congregants were as talented. All of a sudden, an extremely shrill, off-key version of a song came from a voice behind them. Not wanting to seem rude, the folks just kept singing along while fighting the urge to turn around and identify the off-key singer. Being such an inquisitive dog, Marnie didn't have quite the same reaction. At the first startling sounds coming from behind her, Marnie jumped up from her down position on the floor and did what the folks attempted not to do. She swung her head around and stared at the woman behind her who was just singing away as if dulcet tones were coming from her mouth. Marnie noticed that other members of the congregation were looking at the woman as well. Being the kind hearted dog that she was, Marnie didn't want the woman to be embarrassed at the attention. So, Marnie did what only sweet and sensitive Marnie would do...she took a huge breath and enthusiastically joined in the singing. Only Marnie didn't just sing...she howled and howled at the top of her voice. Momentarily startled by the high-pitched sounds and then realizing that the attempt at a duet was coming from Marnie, our dad gave Marnie a subtle leash correction that quickly ended her performance. While thoroughly embarrassed by Marnie's performance, the folks imagined the incident as the howling that was heard around the world. In reality, Marnie's first attempt at a duet merely echoed throughout the entire church and never reached the other side of the front doors!

What the folks didn't see, in their temporary moment of panic and nervousness, was the reaction of the congregation. They were all smiling at Marnie's first attempt at a serenade with violin accompaniment. While Marnie received a slight correction for her impromptu duet in church, in her defense, she was only trying to do a good deed for someone in need...someone in need of serious vocal lessons. There was definitely truth to the saying that no good deed goes unpunished.

As Marnie's training continued, she wasn't at all fearful of being around large groups of people. Since crowds didn't bother her at all, she often accompanied our mom and dad to races supporting various organizations. Dad was a devout runner, entered numerous races sponsored by charitable organizations and always enjoyed seeing Marnie waiting for him at the finish line. One summer morning, they attended a combination Race/Walk/Festival designated for assistance to families having autistic children. Held on a huge farm, the event offered a variety of interesting events. Since it was cooler in the morning, the Race/Walk was the very first event. The runners would start first, and the walkers would follow. Crowds, surrounding the starting line, cheered and applauded as the runners anticipated the sound of the starter pistol signaling the beginning of the race. Marnie couldn't see our dad from her low vantage point, but she knew that he was somewhere in the crowd. The sound of the starter pistol startled Marnie a bit, but she recovered quickly as the runners cheered and laughed as they ran past her location. The walkers followed at a much slower pace, but everyone seemed to be having a good time, and the crowd continued to cheer and applaud.

As soon as the last walker had passed the starting line, the spectators wandered in all directions to pass the time while waiting for the first runner to cross the finish line. Since it would take Dad at least fifteen minutes to complete the race course, our mom and Marnie decided to do a bit of sightseeing on the grounds. Marnie had never been on a farm before and didn't quite know what to expect. They saw a huge barn and decided to do a bit of exploring. Once inside, they saw two rows of enormous, empty horse stalls with buckets of feed hanging from the sides. Bales of hay lined the walkway between the rows, and bridles hung from hooks on walls that were surrounded by photos of the owners and their animals. Not only did Marnie's eyes dart all over the place so as not to miss anything in the barn, her nose was going wild with the stimulating scents. Even though a dog in training for service was not supposed to go sniffing around, our mom allowed Marnie to do it because it was such a new experience. Mom believed that all work and no play made for a very dull dog…and Marnie was never ever close to being dull!

After leaving the barn, they walked past enormous animal pens, all types of intricate-looking farm machinery and finally, a huge vegetable garden. Marnie wasn't able to identify any of the vegetables except corn, but that didn't matter to her. She was just enjoying the sights, sounds and scents. They strolled around a bit more and then made their way to the finish line to greet the winners.

The same crowds that were present at the starting line waited anxiously at the finish line for the first runner to claim the winning trophy. Seeing the first runner come around that final curve in the distance brought cheers of encouragement from the spectators as he raced for the first place award. Once he crossed the finish line, others followed. As if on cue around the fifteen-minute mark, our dad was seen coming around that final curve and approaching the finish line. Marnie wasn't usually a barker at public events, but, this was our dad, and he was running as fast as he could. She had to offer her very own personal version of canine encouragement, and that took the form of loud, nonstop barking. As he heard her excited barking amidst the clapping and the cheering, our dad raced even faster

The Victory Kiss

to the finish line. Because of Marnie's encouragement, he achieved record time for the distance, won a first place medal and owed it all to Marnie. She was so happy to have been a part of his success and gave him a victory kiss at the finish line.

Once our dad cooled down from the rigors of the race and changed his clothes, the folks went off with Marnie to enjoy the festivities. This huge farm had an amusement park set right in the middle of the property. All sorts of rides filled the area, but the Ferris Wheel was the one that caught Marnie's interest. She stood off to the side watching as children handed over their tickets and were locked into basket-like seats. Once the ride started, Marnie was mesmerized as it went around and around amidst the screams of glee from the children as their seats swayed back and forth during the ride. Soon after the ride had begun, Marnie experienced pangs of dizziness and felt that she had seen enough of that ride. She tugged at her leash signaling her desire to move on, and off they went to another part of the festival.

Children had numerous opportunities for amusement. People in colorful costumes were in charge of face painting, clowns made balloon animals, strolling musicians played energetic tunes on their instruments, and a giant man walked in a wobbly manner through the crowd. He was one of the tallest and most unusual-walking men that Marnie had ever seen, but she later learned that he was just an ordinary sized man walking on something called stilts. In Marnie's opinion, this was one precarious way to amuse people. Anyway, Marnie had never experienced any of these things before, and no matter how unusual they were or where they went on the farm, there was always something new and exciting to see or do. It was an incredible experience for Marnie and one that she'd never forget.

As they moved through the crowds, they came to the refreshment area. Attendants, in colorful booths that lined the walkways, sold popcorn, cotton candy, peanuts, hotdogs, ice cream, soda and water. The aromas that filled the air made Marnie's mouth water, and she craved just a small bite of something...anything! She even looked for dropped morsels of food on the ground just to satisfy a tiny bit of her hunger. Unfortunately, this was perhaps the cleanest refreshment area of all times, and Marnie found nothing suitable for eating on the ground.

Just past the refreshment area that was in no way refreshing for Marnie, they went to the areas designated for various demonstrations. The first was an equestrian dressage performance given by specially trained horses and their riders. Marnie had never even seen horses before let alone witnessed such amazing demonstrations of skill and precision. The horses were huge and tremendously powerful. Yet, in spite of their strength and size, they were examples of grace in motion when performing. They were amazing, and Marnie couldn't wait to tell Kessen and Brightie all about them.

The canine agility demonstrations were next, and Marnie was so excited to see dogs of all sizes doing such incredible athletic activities. They flew over hurdles, sailed through tire-jumps, ran through open and closed tunnels, scurried up and down a seesaw and ended with a final leap onto an elevated platform called a pause table. The event was such an unbelievable exhibition of athletic expertise, and Marnie was in awe of the performances. Doing those types of exercises took not only skill and speed but courage as well. She didn't see herself running through any tunnel or over a seesaw any time soon. She preferred keeping her four paws safely on the ground.

Moving past the demonstration arenas, they came close to the end of the festival where small children were enjoying rides on ponies who were attached to a contraption that kept them walking in a circle for the duration of the ride. From Marnie's perspective, the ponies looked significantly bored but walking in a circle all day wasn't necessarily conducive to "laugh out loud" fun. While walking all day, they never did get anywhere. In Marnie's mind, that defeated the purpose of walking in the first place. But, who was she to criticize? After all, the ponies didn't seem to mind, and they were the animals going in circles all day long.

They left the festival right after watching the pony rides, and everyone was tired from the day's festivities. Marnie had an exciting and fun-filled day that held a variety of new experiences. She had so much information to share with Kessen and Brightie when she got home. She didn't realize how exhausted she was until she walked through the kitchen door. She went directly to her kennel, curled up in a comfortable manner and fell sound asleep. She'd share her experiences with Kessen and Brightie in the morning.

The holiday season was approaching, and Marnie was excited to participate in the festivities. Because it was Marnie's first Christmas, she really didn't know what the celebration was all about. Kessen told her that during the holiday season, many interesting events took place. One particular event was having the carolers come to the house. Their neighbor's children would visit homes in the area and sing Christmas carols outside their front door for entertainment. They were called Christmas carolers, and everyone in the neighborhood awaited their arrival each holiday season. After listening to their songs, folks would give each child a special treat for their efforts. Then, the children would go off to the next home and sing other songs. It was something called a tradition, and they even sang when it was snowing or very cold. Having the carolers arrive and sing the Christmas songs signaled the beginning of the season.

One more thing had to be accomplished before the Christmas season officially began...the taking of the annual Christmas card photo. The dogs were grudgingly dressed in some sort of holiday garb and positioned in front of what the folks referred to as their *mini-tree*, a small, tastefully decorated, artificial tree. The tree had graced numerous hospital rooms in the past and brought great joy to the patients who spent their holidays looking at the tiny tree with its sparkling lights and unusual ornaments. The dogs, however, didn't understand the significance of the tree. They only knew that they were dressed in unusual garb, wore bells on their collars and were expected to behave during the taking of the Christmas photo.

However, Marnie's mischievous tendency emerged, and she thought that having three dogs lined up like little soldiers wasn't in keeping with the Christmas spirit. She was going to make this particular Christmas a most memorable holiday. Kessen and Brightie were not aware of what she had planned nor would they have approved if they had known. Actually, Brightie might have approved if she had known, but she wasn't informed of Marnie's intentions. After all, the photo of them was going to grace the Christmas card sent to all of the folk's friends. What was Marnie thinking?

Anyway, Kessen recognized that mischievous look in Marnie's eyes, but didn't quite know what she was going to do. He just hoped for the best possible outcome believing her sophisticated demeanor would overcome her need for mischief. Unfortunately, he was very, very wrong. They were

all lined up and ready for the first photo to be taken. Kessen was first, Brightie was next and Marnie was last. Mom had the camera ready, and Dad stood in the background with special dried liver treats to hold their attention. Just when the photo was about to be taken, Marnie reached over to Brightie and

Marnie was ready for some fun!

grabbed that red and white colorful collar that surrounded her neck. In response to that, Brightie reached over to Kessen and grabbed the collar of the red and white Santa cape that draped his body. Chaos ensued while all three dogs tumbled around and played enthusiastically with each other.

The folks were not pleased at this turn of events. Never in the history of the Christmas card photo had this sort of chaos occurred. Mom, standing with her hands on her hips in the middle of the room, signaled that the fun was over and serious behavior was expected from each of them. The chaos quickly ended, and the dogs were once again lined up for the photo. Only this time, Marnie was in the middle while surrounded by Kessen and Brighie.

The folks really didn't anticipate Marnie's ability to adjust to situations. Just as the next photo was about to be taken, Marnie leaned over onto Kessen's back and thrust her back legs onto Brightie's body. Game on! All three dogs immediately engaged in creative tumbling and ended by running around the room. Once again, only this time with a much harsher look, our mom faced off with them having her hands on her hips. The dogs knew by the look on her face that she had reached the critical breaking point. They were definitely in for some severe punishment once this photo was finally taken.

For the last time, the folks positioned the dogs for the photo. Only this time, Marnie was on the end and wasn't in any position to instigate mischief. Mom made it very clear to Kessen that his main responsibility as the

Marnie knew how to have a good time!

pack leader was to maintain decorum by being next to her, and Brightie's job was to stay out of trouble. Mom meant business this time, and the dogs definitely knew it. The fun was over for them, but from that day forward, their antics were dubbed the Tradition of Turmoil and repeated every year at Christmas card photo time in honor of their sweet Marnie.

About six weeks later, Marnie's time at the sorority house came to an end. Just before the folks took her to advanced training, they went to church for the traditional blessing from the priest. As they left the church, they passed the well-known Holy Water Fountain that held such attraction to the dogs who proceeded her. Taking a drink of water from that fountain never crossed Marnie's mind. She was, after all, sweet and polite Marnie.

After Marnie went off to advanced training, both Kessen

Kessen hoped she'd return.

and Brightie thought about her a lot and missed her presence in the household. For a few weeks, Kessen waited and looked out the front door hoping she'd return, but that day never came. Months later, they heard that she qualified as a service dog and was helping someone in need of assistance...a fitting outcome for her. After all, Marnie liked people a whole lot better than she liked dogs. Maybe she'd even have an opportunity to use her house-cleaning skills in her new job. Anything was possible!

Marnie's stories were inspiring when Kessen first shared them with me, and I did enjoy sharing them with you, the reader. Marnie was and always will be, the polite, considerate and unexpectedly mischievous pup whose face now graced the wonderful Wall of Fame...

Service was her calling.

INTERMISSION

.

Following this afternoon's attempts at storytelling, I'm finding that it's a form of presentation that is very similar to a theatrical show. If presented properly, it offers a variety of entertainment. I certainly hope that my first venture into this particular theatrical arena has provided some opportunities for enjoyment. I believe there were elements of drama, certainly some comedy, a suggestion of mystery and, for the sake of the audience's well-being, not even a mention of singing. For the record, my singing equates to howling, and that would send the audience running for the exits.

Since I'm sparing my audience from any potential auditory discomfort by not even thinking of howling, I do wish

Break Time

to offer a bit of a break in the form of an intermission. It's just an opportunity to stretch one's legs, grab a refreshment or just rest a little while before resuming the entertainment. I, myself, am taking this time to walk around the house, drink some water and see what form of mischief Brightie has gotten into while I was thoroughly involved with my unique form of entertainment...storytelling.

As I leave my kennel, I can't help but think about Kessen. Worrying about his health isn't very productive, but sharing his stories certainly helps pass the time. I glance at the

129

circular clock on the wall to determine how long the folks have been gone, but then I remember that I don't know how to tell time. Knowing how that clock works could provide me with vital information, and not having a clue as to what the symbols mean is frustrating. I definitely need to learn how to tell time, and Kessen is just the right canine to help me with that skill. Surely, he knows how to do that…he knows how to do everything. Because I lack the ability to tell time, my only choice is to resort to the less than accurate method of telling time known as guessing. Since the sun isn't so bright in the sunroom anymore, I estimate that it is about mid-afternoon. That means that the folks and Kessen have been gone for a very long time. While it's a rather vague estimate of time, it's still not a very good sign in terms of his well-being.

In an attempt to stop worrying for a while, I continue my search for Brightie. She woke up about fifteen minutes ago, left her kennel, gulped some water and went wandering through the house. Who knows what sort of mischief she's gotten herself into this time? Without any adult or canine supervision, nothing stands in her way of getting into trouble.

I didn't have to look very far for her and found that she was doing something strictly forbidden in the sorority house. She deliberately committed the unthinkable infraction of our household rules…she jumped onto the couch and found a comfortable resting place. Well, it really wasn't an unthinkable

The Defiant One

act since both of us often dreamt about resting on the couch, but she blatantly defied all semblance of order by actually doing it. Thinking about it and doing it are two entirely different things. Brightie has more to worry about than just consequences from the folks. With that defiant act, Kessen's wrath will come down on her with the speed of fleas jumping onto the back of a feral cat. I guarantee that she'll get more than just the *stink-eye* from him, and I definitely wouldn't want to be in her paws when he finds out what she's doing,

Now, Brightie's act of rebelliousness might not seem all that serious to you, the reader, but in our canine world, rules set up by the folks and especially by the pack leader, are typically followed without question. Truth be told, had I thought of couch-sleeping first, I might have done the same thing and gotten away with it because my black coat wasn't as noticeable as Brightie's blonde hair. Unfortunately, it was a missed opportunity on my part, but in the end, I have total deniability when faced with Kessen's harsh interrogation techniques…and believe me, he is a wizard when it comes to these methods. Rumor has it that he is capable of boring a hole through a dog's head with just the glare from his eyes during one of his interrogations. This time, I'm glad that I didn't engage in the couch caper. I wouldn't make a good suspect since I'd crack faster than an over-ripe nut being eaten by a squirrel, and might I add, I would not look my best with a hole in my head. While I enjoy naughtiness as much as the next canine, I reserve the right to retain pride in my appearance.

What surprises me is that Brightie usually puts some thought into her ventures by first weighing the gains and the losses. Possible consequences usually figure heavily on her decisions to proceed or not. Since Brightie is an never-ending shedder, she apparently put no thought whatsoever into this gambit. That blonde fur of hers is a definite giveaway and will immediately identify her as the culprit. What is wrong with her? Getting caught is a given in this instance, and yet, it doesn't seem to matter to her. I know that for a fact from the sound of her powerful snoring. That depth of sound is only achieved through total relaxation and lack of guilt.

I'm totally safe from blame in this situation since my coal-black coat is my alibi. I feel relieved because between Brightie's gorgeous eyes and that innocent look of hers, she is never the first one blamed for mischief. Even at a very young age, using her femininity as a means of manipulating situations earned her the nicknames of Brightie Girl and Sweet Cheeks. Unless she is caught in the act, she is completely safe from reprisals. I am always the first to be accused of any wrongdoing in the folks' blame game. In all honesty, they are usually correct since my face lacks that distinctive look of innocence. Instead, my expression depicts downright mischief at its finest…right down to the sparkle in my eyes when caught in some form of naughty act. I say this with a pronounced sense of pride and someday hope to be named the Poster Pup for Impish Behavior. As you can tell, my goals are not at all lofty and, at the same time, are somewhat ill-advised.

I enjoyed being a rascal!

The folks insist that I show absolutely no remorse when caught disregarding the rules. According to their observations, I tend to appear very proud of whatever ill-behaved act was committed. What can I say? What would life be without challenges and risks that necessitate digging outside the box? I'm not a complicated canine...I simply enjoy being a rascal, and that is all there is to it.

But today is not the time for thoughts of mischief and mayhem. It is a time for sharing stories and hopes for Kessen's well-being. I am now thoroughly refreshed after this brief intermission and am ready to continue with the so-called entertainment. I saunter back to my kennel because it offers an unobstructed view of the Wall of Fame which, in turn, allows me to select just the right photo for the next story. While I've already shared stories of Turin, Kessen, Brightie and Marnie's escapades, the next story is about the fifth puppy to arrive at the sorority house. She not only alters the serenity of the household, but also gives the folks and the Socialization Squad experiences well beyond their scope of imagination. I hope you enjoy her adventures...

Shall we continue?

133

Izzy

A female, black Labrador Retriever named Izzy was the fifth puppy to come to the sorority house for training as a potential assistance dog. Both Kessen and Brightie, having experienced great success with Marnie as Socialization Squad mentors, were temporarily lulled into a false sense of security and pride in their socialization abilities. They thought that all dogs were as sweet, polite and easily socialized as Marnie. The folks were just as susceptible to those feelings, felt great pride in Marnie's success and looked forward to their next adventure with this new member of their household. Never once did they imagine that so much could go so very wrong in such a short period of time. All members of the family, human and canine, were in for a great surprise.

While Kessen and Brightie waited anxiously at home for the new arrival, the folks braved the ice and snow of the treacherous highways to get to the training facility to pick up their new puppy. Their excitement levels were high as they pulled into the driveway of the training center, and so many questions filled their minds. Would this next pup have the leaping capacity of Turin, the sensitivity of Kessen, the guile of Brightie or the gentleness of Marnie? These past pups were all unique in their own ways, and this next puppy would be just as special. Perhaps, the puppy would have the qualities from each of the previous dogs.

They didn't know too much about this puppy whose name was Izzy other than what they were told. She was a female, black Labrador Retriever...a bit older, petite for her age, very smart and a bit of a jumper. On paper those qualities sounded quite manageable, yet reality was about to smack them right in the face. Upon meeting her, they saw that she was, indeed, a female, black Labrador Retriever...was almost fourteen weeks of age, definitely small in stature and probably smart judging from the eagerness in her eyes. However, the part about being a bit of a jumper was a total underestimation of this pup's ability to jump parallel to the ground from a standing position. Her type of jumping skill was very typical of a Jack Russell Terrier but rarely seen in larger breeds. Izzy had a highly developed skill for such a young puppy. As they would soon find out, the folks weren't at all prepared for this degree of jumping ability. Nevertheless, they welcomed Izzy into their family with high hopes for her future success as an assistance dog. Unfortunately, their hopes and Izzy's dreams were headed for quite a collision.

Knowing that some people were coming to see her, Izzy realized that her life would change drastically if adopted. In her kennel environment, she had no rules to follow and no set schedules. Her time was her own, and she could run, jump and play whenever she felt like it. While having a family was important to her, being a champion athlete was just as important. She wondered if she would be able to have both, and these thoughts caused her to experience unfamiliar feelings of apprehension.

Living in a new environment would probably necessitate following rules, and that would be a distinct challenge for Izzy since she wasn't accustomed to following orders. She faced so many unanswered questions, and she didn't even know what she'd call her new family. Seeing their car pull into the facility's circular driveway and watching them get out of the car, Izzy immediately made some snap judgements.

This new life would be challenging.

The man was rather tall, very handsome and seemed quite cheerful. Because she'd probably have to follow rules, and rules had to be enforced, the name Good Cop immediately popped into her head as she perceived his kind face and gentle manner. She might be able to win him over quickly. But, the woman, on the other paw, was quite a different story. Although she had kind eyes, Izzy sensed a bit of a disciplinarian and stickler for rules in her demeanor. Getting her way with this woman would be a challenge so Izzy named her Bad Cop. These names definitely weren't permanent ones, but they'd have to do for now. Following the couple's completion of the adoption paperwork, Izzy said goodbye to her old way of life and apprehensively entered the new one.

The ride home was periodically interrupted by Izzy's howls and screeches. Apparently, her familiarity with being in a dog crate was nonexistent. But, the folks were used to this behavior when bringing a new puppy home. After all, the world was turned upside down for the puppy and was probably quite frightening. As they traveled on the snow-filled highway, the folks understood how Izzy must be feeling and just wanted to get home safely with their hearing intact.

Four hours later, Kessen and Brightie heard the tires of the car crunching the ice and snow left on the driveway from the previous night's snowfall. The folks were finally home and bringing the new protégé for the Socialization Squad. Their excitement levels were off the puppy charts in anticipation of all of the adventures that they would share with their new puppy. Kessen and Brightie assumed their best sitting position in an effort to demonstrate the proper form of greeting at the door. After all, their mentoring began the moment the puppy entered the sorority house. Little did they know the extent of the unusual surprise that awaited them, and it was all wrapped up into one, really small package.

That pup was fast!

The two eager dogs sat perfectly still as the back door opened. Suddenly, something black in color rushed past them very quickly. It was the new puppy. She offered no suitable greeting, no proper sniffing and within a few seconds was nowhere in sight. This new arrival literally literally stormed the quiet household. After briefly losing traction on the slippery floor, Izzy quickly regained her paw-hold on the floor tiles, gained speed, ran through the kitchen, sailed through the opened gate and began her assault on the house. Halfway down the hall, she knocked over the ceramic, elevated food bowls that, in turn, knocked over the stainless steel water dishes. The noise of the bowls hitting the floor reverberated through the house. The racket from the bowls, however, didn't faze Izzy at all. If anything, it caused her to increase her speed…as if running any faster were even possible at this point. Because she was moving at such a fast pace, she wasn't able to stop fast enough to avoid bouncing off the closed bedroom door at the end of the hall. The impact must have turned her around, or she had a hidden reverse gear in her body because she then made her way back down the hall to the living room…at top speed. Rugs were scattered and pillows were overturned as this black, tornado-like ball of puppy energy circled the room. Her enthusiastic rampage ended with her bouncing off the cabinet in the dining room. This pup sure could bounce! Suddenly, exhaustion overcame her, and she fell asleep in the only untouched doorway left in the house. Her arrival was a complete disaster, and what seemed like an endless assault on the house took only minutes.

Needless to say, no one had ever witnessed such behavior in the sorority house before this pup's arrival. Kessen and Brightie were stunned as were the folks at this display of puppy-induced bedlam. The realization that this puppy would be in residence for the next fifteen months was staggering in its seriousness. Within minutes, Izzy had destroyed several parts of the house…not to mention her bouncing off the walls and doors. The sorority house now had a weapon of mass destruction in the form of a petite, black puppy in residence. Faster than any puppy ever received a nickname, this pup was dubbed the Izz-Manian Devil.

Once the dust finally settled, Kessen and Brightie found a secure hiding place at the other end of the house and had to re-think their approach to Izzy's socialization. Brightie, suddenly bowing to Kessen's authority as the leader of the

pack, decided that because of his position, he was the logical choice to be in charge of the new arrival. It was payback time for Kessen, and he knew it. All of the times that he grinned at Brightie from his position on the forbidden furniture or was

They found a safe place to hide.

protected from blame even though he participated in mischief were coming back to haunt him. Until now, he thought that karma was reserved for the humans of the world. Sadly, being in charge of this little rascal was proof that it also extended to the canine world. Kessen had no choice but to step up to the plate or in his case, the food bowl, and take charge. While he'd never admit this to Brightie, he was a bit frightened by this puppy's initial behavior. His hackles, wildly traveling up and down his back, signaled loud and clear warnings of impending danger. Izzy's presence for the next fifteen months was definitely going to give the household an experience that they would long remember. Nevertheless, Kessen was convinced that once Izzy adjusted to her new environment, she would likely embrace their mentoring and develop some acceptable behavioral skills. While Brightie wanted to believe Kessen's predictions, she was still skeptical and, for the first time, was glad that she wasn't the leader of the pack.

Izzy woke up later that evening and was totally embarrassed by her earlier behavior. She didn't know if that

She had to fix this.

unexpected rampage was due to her fear of not being accepted by this new family, missing her birth mother and siblings or anxiety over the change in her living situation. All she knew was that she made a total fool of herself and probably frightened the residents of the entire house. She questioned how this family would ever accept her after that display of misbehavior. She'd have to find a way to make things right with everyone.

After everybody in the household had gone to sleep, Izzy thought about all of the events of the day. Pangs of loneliness filled her as she thought about missing her birth mother and siblings. Even though Bad Cop had left a night light on for her, Izzy was still frightened because of all of the changes in her life. She felt all alone in a new living situation with two people who were strangers and two dogs who apparently wanted nothing to do with her. Tears filled her eyes as she thought about the losses in her life, and her soft whining turned to earsplitting howling that echoed throughout the house.

Hearing the howling coming from the kitchen, Bad Cop

quickly came to Izzy's kennel. She spoke softly to her and began playing some soothing music on a portable machine that was placed on a stand near her kennel. Bad Cop told her that the songs were canine lullabies set to a mother dog's heartbeat and were meant to relax her on her first night here. Izzy continued to howl even louder, but Bad Cop sensing that Izzy just might need some privacy, covered her kennel walls on three sides with a clean sheet. Izzy now had some privacy and soft music helping her through the first night away from her previous kennel environment. Izzy didn't realize it, but Bad Cop waited on the other side of the kitchen gate until she fell asleep. Bad Cop wasn't as bad as Izzy thought, but Izzy wouldn't know that for quite some time.

When morning came, the couple acted as if nothing had happened. They greeted her cheerfully, gave her an exceptional breakfast, took her for a walk in their huge yard, allowed her to play in the snow and even gave her a few more toys. Izzy was completely lost in terms of what was happening. In spite of her earlier misbehavior, she received only kindness from these people. Izzy was convinced that they were proficient in mind control, and their unusual response had to be a form of mind-messing at an advanced level. She was now certain that she'd have to keep her wits about her in order to survive in this environment.

Izzy saw the two resident dogs looking skeptically at her from a safe distance behind the now closed gate. She was determined to make things right and approached the twosome. On seeing her moving towards them, the smaller of the two immediately stepped behind the taller one. Judging from his discerning look which Izzy would later learn was called the *stink-eye*, she quickly identified him as the pack leader. While she knew that making things right wasn't going to be easy, his penetrating and somewhat scary look indicated that she was about to be the recipient of some well-deserved consequences. She looked up at him with her best attempt at an apologetic expression and introduced herself. Because he was quite tall, Izzy's looking up at him actually put her in a sitting position. She detected a flicker of softening in his eyes and thought that he might have interpreted that gesture as recognizing his authority. Perhaps he was ready to accept an appropriate greeting from her. She did so as best as she could through the rails of the gate. He announced that his name was Kessen, and his position was that of the leader of the pack in this household. That spark of gentleness was now gone from his eyes, and Izzy detected a bit of arrogance in his attitude…not that she was prepared to comment. After all, today was a day to make amends for yesterday's total lack of proper manners. Hopefully, her contrite attitude and remorseful look would work magic toward her goal of reconciliation.

Now, Izzy wasn't quite sure that she could pull that off with this perceptive leader of the pack. He seemed like the type of capable canine who could see through to the back of her head if he so desired. His eyes were extremely penetrating and his demeanor posed a great threat to her well-being if she didn't adhere to the household rules. Izzy was quite troubled since she didn't even know what rules to follow. She was positive that her behavior following her arrival broke quite a few of the rules and acknowledged that her disorderly conduct created a somewhat distressing predicament.

Perhaps meeting the other dog might help make amends

and create a smooth transition into the household. Not being in charge, this smaller dog might be easier to convince. As if on cue, the big dog named Kessen moved to the side allowing the smaller Labrador Retriever to move forward and officially introduce herself. Izzy wondered how the pack leader knew that she was going to attempt a meeting with the other dog. Izzy guessed that he quite possibly had the ability to read minds. If this were true, he not only knew her thoughts about his arrogance but also her pretend remorse. With every passing moment, Izzy was getting deeper and deeper into trouble.

The smaller dog cautiously approached the gate and introduced herself as Brighton. She added that the more casual version of her name was Brightie and was used most of the time unless accused of some type of misbehavior. In this situation, her given name of Brighton was used in a most authoritative tone. Brightie went on to tell Izzy that she hoped yesterday's performance was merely a lapse in judgement since both she and Kessen were now her mentors from the Socialization

Squad and, as such, would be in charge of her for the next fifteen months while she trained for assistance.

Izzy didn't know what the Socialization Squad was nor did she know what mentors were. But, she was willing to cooperate in any way that might soften the effects of yesterday's ill-fated performance.

Izzy had a lot to learn.

However, she definitely had to learn more about the training for assistance that Kessen talked about. These dogs had to be mistaken since her future goal was becoming a champion athlete. They already saw some of her running and jumping skills during her rampage of last night. Looking beyond the destruction, her actions were still quite an exhibition of speed and dexterity. Some form of athletic endeavor was in her future, and nothing would stand in the way of her being successful. All she had to do was figure out which activity was best suited for her skills.

Good Cop, the kind man with the gentle eyes, took her out to the yard a lot and allowed her to run and play in the snow on a long cotton leash. Izzy loved playing in the snow, but she wasn't allowed total freedom in the yard because she was still small enough to fit through the fence rails. After witnessing her ability to reach full running speed within seconds the day before, the leash was the best solution to keeping her in the yard until she grew a bit.

Playing with the resident dogs was her first adventure of the day. So as not to overwhelm

He was so good to Izzy.

her, the folks decided that Izzy was going to play with the dogs one at a time. They were much larger and heavier than Izzy, so the folks wanted play time to be both fun and safe. The pack leader named Kessen was the first to enter the play area in the kitchen. Both dogs "play bowed" appropriately, and the fun began. Izzy was hesitant at first to engage in play with Kessen.

In the kennels, she and her siblings jumped and lunged all over each other, but she didn't know the protocol for playing with a pack leader and wanted to make a good impression. Kessen noticed that she was hesitant at first, so he started with a few playful lunges and air snaps…coming close enough to almost touch, but never touching which was strictly forbidden. He teased her a little bit until she jumped to the challenge. Game on! Since they got a bit carried away for a while with their air snapping and jaw sparring, the folks thought it might be a good idea to switch dogs. Kessen's quick response to his folks' command to leave the area surprised Izzy. She didn't think that he answered to anyone. Apparently, the folks had a bit higher status in the household pack order. Surprisingly, Kessen actually had to listen to someone else. Up until this moment, Izzy thought that he answered to no one…definitely important information for future reference.

Switching dogs was very similar to a relay race. As Kessen left the kitchen play area, Brightie quickly entered as if a bone had been passed from one dog to another. This time, the folks had introduced a toy named Mr. Snake. It was a long, plush toy resembling a snake that had a squeaker in its tail. Mr. Snake's extensive length kept the dog's mouths away from each other while they tugged and played. Brightie enjoyed playing with this toy because there was no threat to her flaxen coat being ruffled in any way. She was, first and foremost, a lady and refused to be seen disheveled in public.

Then, the dogs switched partners again, had more fun running and chasing each other and finally ended with each of them dropping to the floor for some well-deserved nap time. Izzy really enjoyed her first experience playing with these new canines and hoped that they might forget about her escapade of the day before. It would be nice to have friends while adjusting to a new environment and what sounded like numerous rules.

After getting used to each other's company, the dogs spent time together and were only separated when Izzy's excitement resulted in something called the *Lab Goofies*. The *Goofies* included spontaneous, uncontrollable bursts of energy that resulted in her running at full speed with ears back and tail tucked while her body was close to the floor. Because there was no trigger for this behavior, it took onlookers entirely by surprise. Izzy would often unexpectedly break into the *Goofies* and would run around the house at full speed. When she did, Kessen and Brightie just hugged the walls in an effort to avoid being bumped or tousled. Sometimes, she'd even bounce into the walls, doors or appliances because of her inability to stop on the slippery floors. While these episodes weren't as destructive as her arrival, they were unsettling in terms of the household's serenity. The frequency of her episodes often led to her incarceration in the kitchen area. Our mom said that Izzy could bounce off the walls from dawn to dusk when in the kitchen but nowhere else in the house. Bad Cop, in spite of her name, sure had a sense of humor.

Izzy was learning the rules, and once she had a chance to settle into her new environment, Kessen and Brightie held a meeting with Izzy to discuss their plans for mentoring. After all, the Socialization Squad had responsibilities and only had fifteen months to reach their important goals. Kessen explained that throughout Izzy's entire time at the sorority house, he and Brightie would teach such things as socialization with others, appropriatedog to dog interaction, bite inhibition, and acceptable public etiquette. Although many training goals existed, these training exercises were starting points for all puppies…especially those who were destined for careers as helper dogs.

Having heard the words *destined for careers as helper dogs*, Izzy suddenly knew what this family had in mind for her, and it apparently didn't include sports. Because her destiny involved some aspect of athletic achievement, Izzy immediately wanted to halt

They had plans for Izzy.

this discussion. She had winning trophies and award ribbons in mind for her career…not helping others. In Izzy's mind, service was for the *goodie four-paws* of the kennels, but definitely not for her. While her goals sounded extremely shallow, Izzy had her own future planned. However, Izzy was just earning Kessen and Brightie's friendships and didn't want to cause any disruption by telling them of her future plans. She was young but definitely wise. At the appropriate time, she would spring this information on them, and when she did, it would cause quite a disruption in the household. In the meantime, she'd go along with their program.

Izzy was a very observant dog and constantly watched Kessen and Brightie for signs of strength and weaknesses. She needed some advantage when she finally told them her future plans. She could find nothing of great significance that denoted any sign of weakness in Kessen. There was, however, one quirk that intrigued Izzy. While he was the height of strength, grace and reason, he did have an uncanny attachment to a somewhat tattered ring toy. Every day, he grabbed that toy from the toy basket, ran out to the yard, traveled around the perimeter once and then assumed a down position in the grass to chew on his toy. This was Kessen's routine, and it never changed.

Izzy asked Brightie about Kessen's unusual connection to that toy. Upon hearing this specific question, Brightie's eyes widened to saucer-like proportions. She warned Izzy that touching Kessen's toy was strictly forbidden because it was given to him by his sister Kelyn on the day they were separated. Kessen came to the Midwest, and Kelyn went somewhere in the South. The ring toy was the only memento that he had of his sister and, consequently, was his most prized possession. Brightie even said that when he had it in the yard, he only pretended to chew on it because he never wanted to ruin it. Having a family keepsake was undoubtedly a valuable possession, and Izzy was happy for him. Because she knew the story behind this toy, Izzy never dared touch it out of respect for Kessen and the family connection.

One look was enough!

As time passed, Izzy noticed that each dog had a way to get what he or she wanted. Kessen used his steely glare known as the *stink-eye* to maintain order among the pack. He knew everything that went on in the household and apparently had eyes in the back of his head as well. One steely look from

Kessen was enough motivation to end any attempt at misbehavior.

Brightie, on the other paw, mostly used her feminine

Her Sultry Look

ways on members of the pack as well as other dogs in the neighborhood. Blinking her long, curly eyelashes at top speed usually mesmerized the other dogs. What surprised Izzy was that Brightie's eyelash technique didn't create a breeze! Although her look of innocence was helpful for her success, Brightie had an even greater weapon in the "Getting Her Way Gambit." It was appropriately called the temper tantrum. It was a masterful plan, and she, herself, was the weapon. When she didn't get her way, she'd roll on her back, kick up her legs and screech at the top of her lungs. Most recipients of this form of acoustical assault would give in because of the possibility of auditory harm. Brightie's marvelous plan worked quite often...not so much with the folks since they had their own methods of counteracting canine warfare. They mastered the art of ignoring her during her tantrums. Nevertheless, Brightie still utilized that ultimate weapon when necessary and just hoped for the best outcomes. Izzy had to come up with her own personal method of getting her way, and that opportunity presented itself a few weeks later. Izzy attended an obedience class called Puppy Kindergarten that ended with puppy play time. Because it was the best part of the class, all of the pups enjoyed it immensely. The class ended six weeks later, and Izzy quickly moved up into the Puppy Continuing class. Most of her former kindergarten class members were in this class, and each puppy really looked forward to play time. When the energetic pups found out that there was no play time allowed in the advanced classes, Izzy staged a quiet rebellion to win back play time for all of her classmates.

Izzy positioned herself on the floor and refused to move. Her rebellion was short lived and ended abruptly when the trainers, the assistants and even the folks started leaving the facility. They were turning off the lights and were actually going to leave her alone hugging the floor in this darkened facility. Apparently, the enemy was well-versed in the art of puppy refusals. Before the last light was turned

She refused to move!

off, Izzy reluctantly ended her rebellion and walked slowly to the exit door.

The trainer, the assistants and the folks were waiting for her at the door. While no one said anything, Izzy sensed the disappointment in her behavior. They drove home in total silence. Even though Izzy didn't win that war, she still made

Mission Accomplished

an effort to right a wrong...at least in her mind. Her tenacity had to count for something, and suddenly, she realized that her rebellion wasn't a total loss at all. Because of her reluctance to move from that prone position on the training room floor, Izzy now had a method of getting her

151

way. Sure, she had to fine tune it a bit, but she had the time to do it. According to Izzy, anything worth doing was worth doing well. She got that bit of wisdom from Kessen.

When they returned home, Izzy told Brightie all about her silent rebellion. She didn't want Kessen to know what she had done because his world revolved around adhering to all rules and regulations. He'd be appalled if he knew what she had attempted. Brightie thought Izzy's rebellion was exciting and wished that she had witnessed it. Izzy was sorry that she had disappointed the folks, but they didn't seem too upset about it. What Izzy didn't know was that Brightie couldn't keep a secret and told Kessen all about it. In addition to that, the folks actually thought that what Izzy attempted was somewhat funny and had a bit of a laugh about it. Little did they know that their laughter was short-lived. Izzy had more surprises in store for them, and those surprises had refusals written all over them.

After a day of planning, Izzy was ready to launch her first in-house refusal technique. While playing with her toys, she waited for Bad Cop to reach for the leash signaling the daily walk. As she approached Izzy with the leash, Izzy ran and hid at the back of her kennel. That act totally surprised the Bad Cop since Izzy seemed to enjoy walking outside. She tried to entice Izzy to come out, but Izzy wouldn't even budge.

Her First Home Refusal

Bad Cop, choosing her battles wisely, left her alone. Izzy's plan had worked, and now, she would take it to another level.

Later in the day, the folks were going to take her for a car ride. Izzy did come out of her kennel, but when she saw the cape, she once again ran back into her kennel. The folks, not knowing what had gotten into Izzy, just put her cape back on the shelf and went for the car ride without her. Izzy definitely was on to something in terms of getting her way, but it did cost her in terms of enjoyment since she really enjoyed walks outside and especially liked going for car rides.

More thought and planning had to go into this refusal technique. The next day, Bad Cop grabbed Izzy's cape and reached for the leash expecting Izzy to run back into her kennel. Instead, Izzy came out, moved quickly into her cape and once the leash was attached, marched out of the house. The folks were definitely confused by Izzy's behavior, but figured that whatever caused her reluctance the day before was probably forgotten.

Once again, they were in for quite a surprise. Izzy was now being selective in terms of her refusals. She might hug the floor while positioned under a table in a restaurant full of patrons. Little did the patrons know that she was refusing to leave, and the folks were not going to drag a potential assistance dog out of a restaurant. Another refusal incident might occur spontaneously in the middle of the street. Izzy would drop to the concrete and just admire the scenery. At an outdoor cafe, Good Cop ended up carrying her from her crouched position because he was frustrated with her antics. Some days Izzy would refuse to get out of the car...other days she would enthusiastically jump out. She was becoming obsessed with refusal opportunities, but her inconsistency with refusals was her bargaining chip. Because of her strange behavior, the folks were considerably worried about her. As a result, they stopped taking her to various places in an effort to find the basis for her actions.

Kessen and Brightie were worried about her as well and called for a pack meeting to discuss the matter. Kessen tried to explain to Izzy that she was only hurting herself by refusing to do things. She wasn't going for walks, car rides or public outings. He just wanted to know what she was accomplishing by her refusals. When confronted in this way, Izzy really didn't have any valid answers because she really wasn't achieving anything. She admitted that she was obsessed with the power of refusals and compared them to Kessen's and Brightie's methods of getting their ways.

Both dogs looked at each other and burst out laughing. Now, Izzy was really confused and demanded an explanation.

They had a good laugh!

Kessen assumed his serious demeanor and explained to Izzy that he didn't use his steely glare to get his way. He used it to emphasize his position as the pack leader and, more often than not, to serve as a warning to avoid trouble. It wasn't a random act like her refusals. Instead, it was a planned occurrence having a purpose. On the other paw, Brightie's temper tantrums were, at times, successful in terms of getting her way, but each time she drew that type of attention to herself, she lost a bit of something of great importance...her reputation. A reputation was earned, and, once lost, it was most difficult to regain.

Everything Kessen said made sense, and Izzy had to re-think her position on refusals. However, since they were having this serious discussion, Izzy felt it was the right time to discuss her future career plans. Taking a deep breath and assuming a perfect sitting position to denote confidence, Izzy told them that she was not going to be an assistance dog. She had the right to choose her own career and knew, without a doubt, that she was destined to be a champion athlete. While she wasn't sure which athletic activity was best for her, she knew that she had the running and jumping skills to be successful in some form of athletic endeavor.

Kessen was not pleased.

Kessen saw the determination in Izzy's eyes and knew that she was quite serious. For her to approach him with this shocking news took great courage on her part. Brightie, seeing the disappointment in Kessen's eyes, was taken aback by Izzy's newsflash and wondered just how the folks were going to react to this newest information. Izzy had no way of sharing that information with them. They didn't speak the dog's language, and Izzy didn't speak theirs. It was quite a predicament, and one that had never occurred in the sorority house.

Kessen was very clear that his job was to prepare Izzy for assistance, and until she decided to go along with the program, he would have nothing more to do with her. Even though Brightie understood Izzy's position, she had to follow

Kessen's lead. He was the pack leader, and his decisions were final. Izzy was now left on her own in the household. She later learned that her shunning extended to the neighborhood dogs as well. They were all pack members of a sort and, as such, respected the decisions of the pack leader.

Izzy was alone once again even when surrounded by other dogs. She limited her refusals as a means of getting out and about, so her public outings were back on track. The folks didn't know how she felt, and because of that, continued working with her toward assistance. They traveled to numerous public places, charitable functions and dog walks. The dog walks were usually sponsored by assistancece dog organizations, and Izzy had opportunities to meet numerous service dogs who had jobs helping others. They all had a special quality about them, and Izzy felt quite shallow when she shared her own career goals with them.

Surprisingly, not one dog seemed judgmental when she talked about championship status and athletic glory. Their open-mindedness confused her in light of Kessen's staunch disapproval. When asked about their liberal attitude, one rather distinguished Labrador Retriever told her that not every dog wanted to be a helper dog, and not every dog was capable of being one. For an assistance dog to be successful, the dog had to have just the right combination of temperament, commitment, ability and willingness to please. Without those, it was better for the dog to choose another career direction. Since Izzy didn't believe that she had those special qualities, choosing another career direction just might be the right decision for her. That was such sound advice and was just what Izzy needed to hear. Not having the appropriate athletic choice in mind was the problem...a huge problem for her.

A few weeks later, Izzy had some answers in the form of career choices. The folks took her to an outdoor fair that featured demonstrations of canine dock diving, disc catching and agility work. Dock diving was first, and it involved dogs leaping into a huge pool of water after a thrown toy. The winner was the dog who jumped the farthest. That seemed easy enough until Izzy actually witnessed the demonstrations. First of all, the pool was huge and not at all like her bathing tub at home. In addition to that, the water was very deep. The applause was deafening as each dog literally flew across that pool after the toy. She imagined what it would be like to hear that applause for one of her winning dives but quickly did a reality check. Truth be told, she didn't even like getting a bath in shallow water let alone diving into a huge pool of deep water. Dock diving unquestionably wasn't for her.

Disc catching was the next demonstration and was held in a huge field surrounded by a wire fence. She loved watching the dogs leap, twist and fly through the air to catch a thrown disc. Each dog completed the demonstration by leaping onto the back of their handler as the crowd enthusiastically applauded their athletic ability. Izzy was so enthusiastic watching each dog and attempting to imitate their movements that she forgot there was a wire fence in front of her and bounced right into the fence when duplicating a leap. Since the folks were accustomed to having Izzy do odd things, they didn't even question her actions. Izzy was so excited because now she had a possible career direction. Her jumping and twisting skills were incredible, and all she had to do was develop more height and some twisting styles. Izzy knew disc catching was definitely something she could do.

Agility demonstrations were next, and as Izzy watched the dogs jump over hurdles, run through tunnels, dive through hoops and go up and down a seesaw, she discovered another career option. She had the athletic ability to be successful in this sport as well. Now, all she had to do was find a way to make her dreams known to the folks which certainly wouldn't be easy. She would need Kessen and Brightie's help to accomplish this, but the greater challenge was for Izzy to get back into Kessen's good graces.

As your storyteller, I must momentarily deviate from the story for a point of clarification. What follows is Kessen's version of a weekend's activities as verified by Izzy. Because of my personal involvement in this particular weekend, I choose to relate the events as told to me by Kessen. This approach maintains the integrity of Kessen's version and, at the same time, allows no opportunity for personal bias. I'm strictly adhering to my responsibilities as the storyteller at my own personal expense and my reputation.

Izzy's opportunity for redemption arose as a result of a

The Weekend Visitor

weekend spent with a visiting puppy named Tansy. Following Izzy's decisions to pursue either disc catching or agility competition, she spent her yard time developing her speed and jumping skills. While Kessen and Brightie were still avoiding her, they continued to watch her as she worked tirelessly at improving her skills. While pretending to play a game of tug with Brightie and Mr. Snake, Kessen took note of Izzy's efforts and was most impressed with her perseverance. He decided to give Izzy one last opportunity to re-join the pack as well as gain his support for her dreams. A puppy named Tansy was coming to the sorority house for the weekend, so Kessen decided to put Izzy in charge of her welfare.

Since Tansy's foster family weren't able to pick her up, our folks offered to travel to the training facility to get her and keep her for the weekend. They surprised Kessen, Brightie and Izzy by taking them along for the ride. Upon their arrival, our mom went in to get Tansy and about fifteen minutes later came out carrying that little, black bundle named Tansy. Rather than ride in the canvas crate in the back of the car, Tansy rode on our mom's lap and, much to everyone's surprise, slept all the way back to the house.

Because Tansy seemed like such a calm puppy, Kessen was glad that he put Izzy in charge of her for the weekend. Izzy was encouraged by Kessen's trust in her and felt that perhaps he was changing his position on her dreams of athletic glory. With this hope in mind, Izzy was determined to make a success of the weekend. After all, Tansy was just a puppy and probably easily intimidated. These were Izzy's thoughts…until she met the wide-awake version of Tansy.

For the next two days, Izzy was chewed on, chased, jumped on, bumped, pushed, licked and harassed by a nine week old, energetic Labrador Retriever. Being in charge was much more difficult that Izzy had anticipated. She also gained a newly discovered appreciation for Kessen's job as pack leader. By the end of the weekend, Izzy was exhausted but had successfully managed to keep Tansy out of serious trouble with one important exception…the ring toy caper. Tansy had done a forbidden act, but Izzy resolved the problem. Izzy never

spoke about the incident but was happy to see Tansy leave in the same condition as her arrival. That bundle of energy left walking on all four legs, had all of her teeth and no bites or bruises on her body. As far as Izzy was concerned, it was quite a successful weekend endeavor, and she was quite proud of her successful first attempt at

Puppy sitting was exhausting!

puppy sitting.

As a token of his appreciation for a job well done, Kessen presented Izzy with a plastic disc that had been given to him as a present from a group of students. Rather than just jumping into the air after an imaginary disc, Izzy finally had a real disc for her workouts. Kessen now realized how serious Izzy

Good Job!

was regarding her career choices and offered his support. So, Izzy was welcomed back into the pack. Brightie was delighted with Kessen's change of heart as well as the neighborhood dogs' decisions to follow Kessen's lead.

Happy Days

These were very happy days for Izzy. She had Kessen's approval, her extra-special disc for practicing her catching techniques and the memory of a successful puppy sitting venture with Tansy. But, Izzy's enjoyment of her success was short-lived. Two weeks later, the foster family having Tansy suffered a family crisis and weren't able to keep Tansy for the training months. Our folks, who were always willing to help, offered to take Tansy for the duration of her training. So, Tansy came back to the sorority house and not just for a visit. Kessen and Brightie looked forward to having another new puppy for their Socialization Squad's mentoring, and Izzy searched for better hiding places both inside and outside of the house. Izzy had a number of canine friends in the neighborhood and was happy when they resumed their visits. One dog in particular, a chocolate-colored Labrador Retriever named Finnegan, started out as quite a thorn in her paw pad when they were introduced. He was brash, arrogant, bold and maintained the title of Neighborhood Dog's Dog. The male dogs envied his sleek,

He was a handsome dude!

muscular build that didn't show an ounce of any body fat...probably the result of his working out a lot. The females, with the exception of Izzy, watched how his glossy coat emphasized his muscular build as he raced through the yards. Watching Finnegan strut his stuff was quite an event that caused all of the neighborhood female dogs to drool at the possibility of being his girlfriend. Izzy thought that they were all just being ridiculous. After all, Finnegan was basically just another dog. Granted, he was very handsome in a rugged sort of way as well as a testament to living a healthy lifestyle. Nonetheless, he was still just another dog in the neighborhood. Izzy didn't have time for pooch watching and drooling. She had plans for athletic glory and couldn't be bothered with such silliness.

Finnegan knew everybody, claimed to know how to do everything and was quite proud of his title. Izzy was not at all impressed with him the first time they met. He was running around the perimeter of the fence and was fiercely sniffing the ground in search of prey. Instead of properly introducing himself, he just bellowed out his choice of the special nickname of Toots for her instead of her real name. She was accustomed to Kessen's gallantry and insistence on politeness at all times. Finnegan's brazen behavior and lack of proper etiquette was appalling. To top it all off, he didn't even stop to acknowledge her and just said something about meeting later when he had the time. Brightie told Izzy that Finnegan was just teasing her and wanted to get a rise out of her. Well, according to Izzy, he accomplished his goal and the possibility of meeting her later was a figment of his imagination.

A few days later as Izzy was practicing her jumps, she heard Finnegan making his way from his house to hers. Taunting her with the nickname of Toots as he approached, he took a giant leap, landed right into the yard and stood next to her. At first, Izzy was a bit startled by his airborne arrival, but once she caught her breath, she was no longer surprised by his attempt at a dramatic arrival. He gave an appropriate greeting, apologized for his rude behavior the other day, mentioned that teasing was his favorite form of fun and hoped that they might see a lot of each other. He almost had her believing that he was

Izzy secretly thought he was cute!

sincere until he told her that she sure was one lucky female because he picked her, and someday they were going to become the best of friends. Izzy just chuckled at his impertinence, turned around and walked back into the house. She admitted that aside from his not-so-funny jokes along with his exasperating arrogant demeanor, he was pretty cute in a strange sort of way.

From that day on, Finnegan stopped by at least once a day to tease Izzy in some way. He'd call her either Toots or Honey mainly because it seemed to infuriate her. However, when he didn't show up, Izzy actually missed seeing him. He was fun in a goofy sort of way and was gradually winning her over in terms of being friends. Finnegan didn't know that, and Izzy certainly wasn't going to tell him either. Truth be told, she enjoyed his pursuit of her friendship and wanted to keep him guessing about winning it. She had some clever moves of her own and enjoyed using them on Finnegan.

One night, during her last visit to the dog run before going to bed, Izzy noticed that the gates for both the dog run and back yard were left open. This was most unusual since they were usually closed and locked. While there was a small light shining in the dog run, there were no lights in the main part of the huge yard. She moved cautiously through the dog run and entered the darkened yard. Moonlight streaming through the tree branches was the only source of light which made the situation even scarier. While slowly walking through the darkened yard, her hackles suddenly sprung up from neck to tail signaling danger and sending a chill through her body.

With only partial moonlight as a means of seeing anything, Izzy now realized that she was in danger and immediately stopped in her tracks. She sensed something behind her, and as she turned around, a pair of greenish, glowing eyes stared at her from under the protection of an overgrown bush. It moved slowly toward her in a crouching position while emitting a low,menacing growl. As it came closer, the light from the moon identified the creature. A full-grown, scruffy coyote had gotten into the yard through the opened gates.

Izzy was frozen in her tracks as the coyote moved closer to her. She knew that she was no match for that creature in terms of strength but realized that she'd have to defend herself in some way. She couldn't call Kessen and Brightie for help since they were in the house and didn't even know that she was in danger. Because she was in the middle of the yard and the coyote was between her and the house, she had no way of escaping.

Suddenly, Izzy heard the sound of ferocious barking coming closer to the yard from the other side of the fence. Still frozen from fear and unable to move, Izzy watched as Finnegan jumped over the fence, landed in the yard and quickly stepped directly in front of her in order to shield her from from the vicious coyote. Finnegan and the coyote just stared into each other's eyes and with teeth barred were prepared to fight. Finnegan, showing no fear at all, was more than willing and able to go to battle with this coyote. The coyote sensing Finnegan's intent and distinct ability to tear him to shreds with those enormous teeth, turned and ran through the unlocked gates toward the protection of the nearby field.

Once Izzy regained her composure, she thanked Finnegan for risking his life for her. He boasted that he had done things like that a million times and just happened to be in the right place at the right time. When he said that, Izzy knew that he was just being his own silly self. She knew that he had to have sensed that she was in trouble which is why he came leaping over the fence. Nevertheless, he risked his life for her and also gained status as her hero. Sounding a bit humble, which was not at all typical of Finnegan, all he asked in return for saving her life was her friendship. Izzy was more than ready and willing to accept his terms. She did, however, ask him why he came leaping over the fence when he could have come through the opened gates. He mentioned that saving a damsel in distress necessitated a very dramatic entrance. That was so very characteristic of Finnegan!

After Kessen learned about Izzy's brush with danger and Finnegan's rescue, he made a point of thanking Finnegan and assured him that he was welcome to visit the sorority house any time. Izzy just rolled her eyes after Kessen offered him such a generous gift of hospitality.

Finnegan became an invited guest!

165

Finnegan was extremely grateful for the opportunities for more visits and did occasionally stop by while traveling around the neighborhood. He just couldn't resist teasing her and especially enjoyed seeing her face go rigid when he'd call her Toots or Honey. Izzy really didn't mind his teasing, but she couldn't let him know that. If she did, he'd find more ways to torment her.

They definitely had formed a kind of friendship even though it was a bit of a strange one. As a result of her brush with danger and Finnegan's heroics, Izzy became an instant celebrity among the female canines of the neighborhood. She had managed to get Finnegan's attention and didn't even have to drool to win him over. Izzy rolled her eyes in disbelief when she heard that tidbit of gossip. The only thing that she'd ever drool over was a soup bone filled with delicious marrow!

The days passed following her dangerous encounter with the coyote. While practicing her jumping for disc catching competition, Izzy's dreams of athletic glory faced another setback. She was now a year old, very muscular and unable to jump as high as during her younger days. She had to face the stark reality of the situation. Because of her size and weight, disc catching competition was no longer a practical option. It took a while for her to accept that fact, but once she did, she put that plastic disc in the toy basket and never played with it again.

Izzy wasn't herself lately.

The folks noticed that Izzy wasn't her energetic self and wasn't going out in the yard to jump and twirl around as she usually did. Instead, Izzy just hung around her kennel in the kitchen. They thought that a play date was something that would change her attitude, and they knew just the right people to contact for that. Remembering how Izzy had intently watched the agility demonstration at the festival, they rented some agility equipment and set it up in the yard. Izzy was ecstatic when she saw what the folks had done, but then she got an even better surprise. Standing at the gate with his handler was the most handsome Golden Retriever that she had ever seen. His name was Riggins, and when their eyes met, it was love at first sight. Kessen and Brightie noticed that love was in the air along with some serious exercise. This was going to be some special play date.

After the dogs got acquainted, the folks and Riggins' handler took the dogs through the agility course one at a time.

Brightie was fantastic!

It was such great fun for all of them. Izzy tried to do her best to impress Riggins, and he did the same. Kessen spent most of his time on the pause table since he felt that his position was more of a neutral, supervisory role. Brightie, on the other paw, was so incredible in terms of her speed and knowledge of the course. She and Kessen had taken an agility class a few years ago so she knew what she was doing. They went through the course a few times and then took time to rest. After a while, Riggins had to leave with his handler, but both he and Izzy knew that they would see each other again. The folks noticed how much Izzy enjoyed the agility play date and decided to enroll her in an actual agility course. Izzy couldn't believe that the folks knew she was interested in this type of competition. Her dream was finally coming true. Agility was definitely something that she could do, and her size and weight wouldn't stop her from succeeding.

Between going to agility classes and public outings with the folks, Izzy was always busy. She discovered that she looked forward to working in public just as much as going to her agility class. Meeting so many impressive graduate dogs at various outings and hearing them tell of their adventures while helping others in need

Riggins

was causing some doubts in Izzy's mind about her future career choice. Thoughts that maybe assistance to others was a better career choice for her than athletic glory filled her waking moments. When she asked both Kessen and Riggins about her dilemma, both dogs told her to follow her heart. While she really wanted them to tell her what to do, in her heart, she knew that the decision was hers to make and hers alone.

During the next few weeks, Izzy had to make some significant choices. She had a major agility competition coming up as well as the special opportunity to enter into advanced training for assistance. Decisions had to be made, and her time was running out. She had to face leaving the sorority house and everyone who was dear to her. Even leaving Riggins would be a great loss as they had become quite close in the past weeks. Perhaps the outcome of this agility competition would be the deciding factor. After all, she was extremely good at agility yet totally prepared for entering the advanced training program.

The week before her decisions had to be made, the folks took Izzy on a trip down memory lane by visiting all the places they had gone during her stay with them. Friends wanted to see her for the last time and say their goodbyes to her. In spite of her wacky behaviors, frequent incidents of the *Lab Goofies* and temporary obsession with refusals, people really liked her and wished her well in her future endeavors. Seeing their smiling faces and remembering the wonderful experiences she had with them now caused even more doubts in her mind. Going to the church service for the last time and being blessed by that wonderful priest caused her mouth to go dry from emotion. Seeing the famous Holy Water Fountain that challenged each dog to take a gulp brought back a smile to

It was a difficult decision.

Izzy's face. She had done a lot of silly things while in training, but she wasn't about to get caught trying to steal an enormous gulp of water...specifically from a Holy Water Fountain in a church. After all, she did have some standards and doing that would definitely cross the line.

Wanting to make the best possible career decision for herself

169

yet not wanting to give up her dream of athletic glory, Izzy did the best that she could in the competition knowing that the outcome would have some impact on her decision. While waiting for the results of the competition, Izzy thought of her youth and remembered that petite, smart puppy who was a bit of a jumper living in the kennels…the one who had dreams of athletic glory. That puppy was now an adult dog, living her dream yet taking pride in wearing her assistance cape and helping others.

At that very moment in time, Izzy made her choice and the very next day went off to advanced training for assistance work. For most of her young life, Izzy dreamt of achieving athletic glory, yet none of that seemed important anymore. She actually won the competition with fantastic scores, and the folks placed her trophy in a special place on the fireplace mantle. After Izzy left, Brightie found the first place, blue ribbon hanging on the wall of her kennel as a token of their friendship. It was positioned on the proper wall in total compliance with

Izzy looked to the future.

her belief in feng shui, and Izzy knew that would make Brightie extremely happy.

Izzy was confident that she made the right career decision and, after months of advanced training, went on to be successful at helping others. She never once regretted her decision, enjoyed a rewarding life of service and owed it all to two very special dogs…Kessen and Brightie. Through their special mentoring, she learned how to trust her instincts and, above all, to follow her heart.

Izzy definitely made an impact on all members of the sorority house. Steadfastly pursuing her dream of being a champion athlete in a special household that trained dogs for assistance was actually a most difficult challenge for her, but her determination to succeed, against all odds, overcame any and all obstacles. Her strength of character was an inspiration to all who knew her and shared her life. Not only did Izzy earn her place on the Wall of Fame, but she also had a book written about her adventures.

After Kessen shared Izzy's stories with me, I mentioned what wonderful tributes both honors were to Izzy, and it's possible that someday a book might even be written about my escapades. With a bit of a twinkle in his eyes, Kessen looked directly at me and told me that any book written about me would definitely have to be a comic book...

Izzy had an incredible journey.

Tansy

Since very little sunshine is streaming through the windows of our sunroom, I guess that it is pretty late in the afternoon. I can't imagine what is taking the folks so long and why they aren't home by now. At this point, my concern for Kessen's well-being is at the level of out and out worry. Although sharing Kessen's stories is a diversion for me, I sense that something is very, very wrong.

Brightie awakened from her deep sleep on the forbidden couch and immediately committed yet another offense. She jumped off the couch that was newly decorated with blonde hair and jumped onto the loveseat. I can't imagine what has gotten into that dog. Perhaps defiance of the house rules by sleeping on forbidden furniture is her way of dealing with the stress of Kessen's being gone for so long. Personally, engaging in deliberate acts of disobedience that guarantee consequences, seems like a very strange way to deal with stress. When questioned about her behavior, she told me that she just wanted to be alone with her thoughts and didn't care about the consequences. Her innocent face and curly eyelashes weren't going to protect her this time. Staying in my kennel is my solid alibi. For once, I am not in a position to be blamed for the blonde dog hair on the furniture.

Brightie settled into a comfortable spot in the corner of the loveseat and immediately fell asleep. Since worrying about Kessen wasn't going to bring the folks home any faster, I resumed my search on the Wall of Fame for the next subject of my storytelling efforts. I'd like to say that I saved the best for last, but that wouldn't be accurate since it wasn't the final story of the afternoon. It was, however, one that was very close to my heart.

Staring back at me, from what I considered a position of honor, was a stunning, coal-black Labrador Retriever who happened to be the sixth dog to come to the sorority house for training. This gorgeous canine shared an uncanny resemblance to your storyteller, and surprise of all surprises, her name was Tansy...and still is because that is my picture, and this is my story.

When I selected this picture, my first thought was to tell it from my point of view. After all, I was in the best position to tell my story but decided in order to maintain the integrity of Kessen's stories, most of them should be told exactly as he told them to me...from his point of view. Besides, my tendency toward exaggeration pretty much guaranteed some personal bias, and Kessen definitely would not approve. Such a tendency is not characteristic of a good storyteller, and his stories are not only accurate but also told without any personal bias. As far as I am concerned, his rules are my rules as well.

Tansy's story began even before she came to the sorority house. It all started when the folks noticed that the atmosphere had somehow changed. As a result, the interaction among Kessen, Brightie and Izzy was nonexistent. In the past, all three of the dogs played energetically in the house as well as in the yard. Lately, the house lacked the usual chaos of three dogs living together. Nevertheless, the dogs were in for a treat since they were going to have a visitor for the weekend...a puppy named Tansy.

The folks, doing a favor for Tansy's foster family, traveled to the training facility to pick her up and chose to take all three dogs with them. They thought that it made a nice transition for the puppy as well as for the pack members if they met on neutral ground. They would also have some time to get to know each other on the four-hour ride home. Perhaps having the dogs along might even prevent the newcomer from howling and barking. The folks thought of everything and always hoped for the best.

Since all three dogs rarely traveled together, getting them into the car was quite the challenge. With each dog vying for a comfortable position, chaos ensued until Kessen put a stop to the commotion. Kessen designated the middle area of the backseat for his seating pleasure. From that vantage point, he could see clearly out of the front window and knew exactly where they were going at all times. Brightie settled on the right side of the back seat, and Izzy landed on the left. Kessen explained to them that if they stayed in the same spot on the way home, they would see what they missed on the way going to the facility. That made a lot of sense to Brightie and Izzy, and once again, they were amazed at the extent of Kessen's knowledge. He knew everything about anything

After an uneventful yet pleasant trip, they arrived at the training facility. The dogs tumbled out of the car to stretch their legs while our mom went in to sign the necessary papers and bring the newcomer out to greet them. The puppy was a black, female Labrador Retriever named Tansy. To Kessen's dismay, yet another female was coming to the sorority house...even if it were just for the weekend. Kessen tried to shake off the flashbacks from Izzy's arrival with thoughts of Marnie's good conduct, but that was only a temporary fix. However, being the leader of the pack had its distinct advantages since he needed a puppy sitter for the weekend, and Izzy needed a way to get back into the pack's good graces. Kessen decided to give Izzy the opportunity to win back her place in the pack by showing him that she could handle this puppy with ease. Upon hearing of this opportunity, Izzy was ecstatic over the possibility of regaining her position in the pack and readily agreed to take on the responsibility of puppy sitting for the weekend. Once again, the pack leader came through with the perfect solution to all of their problems.

With their eyes locked on the front door of the facility, the dogs anxiously waited for their weekend visitor. Finally, our mom came out carrying a little, black puppy who looked quite comfortable in our mom's arms. Dad brought the dogs out one at a time to greet Tansy. After everyone greeted each other properly, Kessen explained his position as leader of the pack as well as the protocol of the pack order to Tansy. At first, she seemed to listen attentively to Kessen's words, but after a few minutes, her eyes glazed over denoting boredom. Tansy wasn't entirely to blame since puppies have the attention span of a gnat. Not at all offended by Tansy's lack of interest, Kessen continued explaining his expectations of behavior for the weekend. Brightie and Izzy just stifled their laughter and couldn't wait to get into the car.

Once the instructions were completed, Kessen, Brightie and Izzy jumped into the back seat of the car and returned to their original seating arrangement for the ride home. Mom chose to have Tansy ride with her in the front seat rather than in the dog kennel positioned in the back of the car. The return trip went very well since Tansy slept the entire way home to the sorority house.

Judging from her sleep habits, Tansy seemed to be quite a calm puppy. Kessen was pleased that he had given the care

Tansy seemed quite calm.

of this little rascal to Izzy as a means of redemption. Judging from Tansy's behavior so far, this puppy wasn't going to be a problem for Izzy, and her redemption was a safe bet. As it turned out, Kessen wasn't quite correct in his assessment of Izzy's potential success at puppy sitting as well as Tansy's behavior as a weekend guest.

Tansy suddenly woke up when the family reached the sorority house, and it was apparent from her enthusiastic entrance to the house that the car ride home might be the last and only time that she intended to sleep. Having greeted the three dogs earlier at the training facility, Tansy felt no need to repeat the process. Kessen informed her that Izzy would be her mentor for the weekend and would help her enjoy her weekend at the sorority house. Tansy really didn't know what Kessen was talking about since all she really cared about was having a good time. Known as the *party pup* by her littermates, she lived up to her name at every opportunity. For Tansy, this particular day was just the beginning of a special party that would

The Party Pup

probably last the entire weekend, and Izzy, as her mentor, was apparently her *go-to-girl* in charge of fun and entertainment. With that in mind, Tansy rushed out to the yard with Izzy close behind. Kessen found a comfortable spot in the sunroom to watch Izzy's progress, while Brightie developed a plan to stay out of Tansy's way.

As if battery-powered, Tansy ran loops around the yard at top speed. Izzy watched from the safety of the deck in hopes that Tansy would eventually tire herself out from all of the running, but nothing seemed to slow her down. Izzy was going to have her paws full with this little rascal and needed to get this puppy under control in order to regain her position in the pack. Izzy asked herself what Kessen would do in this situation and came up with the perfect answer. Izzy would have a conference with Tansy and discuss proper guest behavior etiquette. Surely, that was a plan that had possibilities.

Izzy enthusiastically ran out into the middle of the yard to share this great plan with Tansy, but unfortunately, Tansy thought Izzy wanted to join in the fun. She chased Izzy all over the yard, zigzagged around shrubs and bushes in an effort to catch her. She even ran the perimeter of the yard between the shrubs and the fence line ignoring the thorny branches. She finally cornered Izzy who was hiding behind the huge lilac bush.

Tansy, not even breathing heavily from the exertion, saw that Izzy was exhausted, had settled in the grass and was panting heavily from all of the running around. Tansy attributed that lack of energy to Izzy's age. After all, her mentor had to be at least a year old, and that bordered on ancient in Tansy's eyes. She let Izzy rest a bit before getting into the party mood again. She had the entire weekend to play…party on girl!

Brightie found Kessen in the sunroom, and together they watched Izzy's situation. Feeling a bit sorry for her,

Kessen didn't interfere.

Kessen actually thought about going out to the yard and stopping Tansy from running around Izzy. However, he had given Izzy a task and hoped that she would rise to the occasion, get the puppy under control and ultimately rejoin the pack. He decided to let Izzy get control of Tansy in her own way and in her own time. Besides, the weekend had only just begun.

The folks, seeing how exhausted Izzy was, rushed into

the yard. Tansy was trying to simulate a mountain climbing expedition. Unfortunately, Izzy was the mountain! Tansy was all over Izzy and wasn't even close to being tired. Watching Tansy in action was a bit like seeing Izzy's arrival all over again...only Tansy's mayhem was outside, and the risk of damage was minimal. However, the folks decided to take pity on Izzy whose head was tucked under and protected by her paws from Tansy's jumping antics. Dad managed to grab Tansy while in mid-air as she jumped over Izzy's body one last time. Seeing that she was now safe, Izzy looked at the folks with love and devotion in her eyes. They had come to her rescue, and she'd be forever grateful for such an act of kindness. Kessen still had high hopes for Izzy's success, and Brightie was now more determined than ever to find a good hiding place in case Tansy got bored with Izzy and came looking for her.

Tansy, on the other paw, was having the time of her life. She knew that Izzy was a bit disappointed by her lack of control, but that really wasn't a concern for her. It wasn't her fault that Izzy didn't have the skills to keep her in line. Now, that other dog...the big one, who claimed to be the pack leader, didn't seem to have a sense of humor. Since she saw the authoritative glare in his eyes when they first met, she immediately

She was ready to rock and roll!

knew that he wasn't easily fooled. In fact, he just might be quite the party pooper, so she would definitely stay out of his way. Because she hadn't seen the other dog named Brightie since her arrival, Tansy felt that the smaller, blonde dog presented no threat to her weekend of frolicking. She was ready to rock and roll with her *go-to-girl* named Izzy.

Izzy spent the night thinking of what approach to use on Tansy. The counseling conference wasn't successful, so she'd have to resort to Plan B...bribery. It worked on Brightie so it quite possibly might work on Tansy. When all was quiet in the household, Izzy put her plan in motion and placed a group of her treasured toys next to Tansy's kennel. When Tansy woke up, she would be so grateful for the gifts that she'd do anything asked of her during the entire weekend. According to Izzy, it was a plan destined for success...but was it?

When Tansy woke up the next morning, she saw the

Squeak toys were boring!

stuffed squeak toys placed outside her kennel. Each toy was just begging for a good squeak and a chew. She'd be happy to play with them once she had her breakfast, but first she had to find Izzy. A party needed to be planned, and Tansy wanted Izzy's help to get that party started. Feeling very confident, Izzy waited to see the expression on Tansy's face when she found the toys. A successful venture in mentoring her first time around would certainly impress Kessen. Now, all she had to do was wait for Tansy to find her and thank her for the gifts. Izzy totally underestimated Tansy's desire for the squeak toys.

Why would she need the squeak toys when she had her very own personal, animated chew toy named Izzy?

Tansy played with the toys for a little while, but eventually got bored with them. She went off to find Izzy to get this mentoring business started. As she walked through the kitchen, she happened to see a rather large ring toy sticking out of a toy basket. Tansy was intrigued by this toy and wondered why Izzy hadn't given it to her with the others. Just as she was about to grab that ring toy, Izzy ran into the room and positioned herself between Tansy and the toy basket. She instructed Tansy that she was never to touch that toy since it was Kessen's special toy, and everyone in the pack had to respect his wishes.

Tansy pretended to observe Izzy's warning and started toward the entrance to the yard. Just as Izzy turned away, Tansy doubled back, grabbed that ring toy and scurried to the yard. Izzy, thinking that Kessen would never forgive her for not protecting his toy, saw her life flash before her eyes. She had to retrieve the toy from Tansy and snatch it before Kessen saw it was missing. Izzy rushed into the

Tansy ran to get the toy.

yard, saw Tansy waiting with the toy dangling from her mouth and ran after her.

Little did Izzy know that Kessen and Brightie had seen Tansy run out to the yard with the ring toy in her mouth, but

Kessen was determined to let Izzy solve this problem. It definitely was a huge problem as far as Kessen was concerned especially if the toy got damaged in the process. Instead of stepping in, Kessen watched intently from the sunroom windows and had faith in Izzy's ability to get his toy back in good condition. Brightie hoped that Izzy would outsmart this ill-mannered visitor so she and Izzy could be friends again as pack members. She missed sharing secrets with Izzy and hearing about her dreams and hopes of athletic stardom.

Tansy, being so much younger than Izzy, knew that she could outrun and even outmaneuver her with this game of Catch Me If You Can. As soon as Tansy saw Izzy come flying out of the house, the chase began. They zigzagged all over the yard and finally came to a stop when Izzy assumed a resting position in the yard. Thinking that Izzy was attempting to catch her breath, Tansy moved closer to her while dangling the ring toy in her mouth. All Tansy wanted was a good game of Tug of War. If she could entice her into playing, Izzy could have Kessen's raggedy, old toy back.

But, Izzy just stared at her and curled her lip while flashing a bit of her adult, strong teeth in a menacing way. Tansy wasn't sure what Izzy was doing, but it looked quite funny. Tansy thought that Izzy was smiling at her and started to laugh. Ignoring the laughter, Izzy added a low growl to the curled lip which only made Tansy's laughter intensify to howling. Once her howling ended, Tansy moved a bit closer, and Izzy not only curled her lip but growled in a low tone while adding a muffled snap in her direction. Tansy did not know what was going on and thought that Izzy was having some sort of medical episode. She thought that Izzy attempted to trick her, but when Izzy put her head down as if to admit defeat, Tansy knew that she had won.

Tansy was thrilled with her ability to outwit this older

Izzy saved Kessen's toy!

dog, and just as she began barking her victory, Izzy swung around and grabbed the toy as it fell from Tansy's mouth. Izzy ran through the yard, onto the deck and into the sunroom where Kessen was waiting. Assuming a respectful sitting position in front of Kessen, Izzy dropped his precious ring toy to the floor in front of him. Izzy had done well as far as Kessen was concerned and had regained her position in the pack.

In the mean time, Tansy came running into the sunroom at full speed in an attempt to get the toy from Izzy. She didn't know that Kessen had been watching the entire incident. As she skidded to a stop on the slippery floor, Kessen stepped in front of Izzy and positioned himself in front of Tansy. Brightie and Izzy were excited because Kessen was about to give Tansy the *stink-eye* and for once, they weren't going to be the recipients of Kessen's intense glare.

Tansy immediately knew that she was in trouble and assumed a sitting position in front of Kessen. He reminded her that she was a guest in the sorority house, and proper canine etiquette was to be followed at all times. If that posed a problem for her, he could arrange to have her remain in her kennel for the rest of the weekend. Tansy wasn't sure that he'd do that, but that spine-chilling glare in his eyes made her believe that it was a distinct possibility. She apologized for her behavior and agreed to conduct herself as a proper guest. Izzy thought that Tansy had her back paws crossed when she talked to Kessen, but she wasn't going to snitch on her. After all, she was just a puppy, and everyone knew that puppies did foolish things.

The rest of the day went fairly well. Tansy enjoyed playing with Izzy although she continued to run, jump, bump and chew on Izzy whenever she could. Her sharp, baby teeth were definitely weapons, and Izzy only had to remind her once that her own adult teeth were much stronger than a puppy's. It was a reminder that Tansy would not soon forget.

The next day, Tansy's foster family came to pick her up,

and as much as Tansy had calmed down, Izzy was happy that she was leaving. Her weekend of mentoring had its ups and downs, but both puppy and mentor had survived. Before Tansy left, she asked Izzy what she was

Tansy was calmer now.

doing in the yard yesterday with the curling of her lip, low growl and muffled snap. Izzy explained that it was part of a Three Step Action Plan taught by a dog named Linus. He specialized in the socialization of rambunctious puppies, and each dog at the sorority house had spent time with him. Tansy was impressed, but reminded Izzy that there was more to what happened than just three steps. Izzy had pretended to give up the fight for the toy and then, unexpectedly, grabbed the toy from her. With great pride in her voice, Izzy admitted that she came up with her very own Fourth Step, and it worked.

Tansy was really saddened to leave the sorority house. In spite of her boisterous behavior, each of the dogs was very nice, and she wished that she had more time to get to know them. Maybe they would meet again sometime...anything was possible. Kessen, Brightie and Izzy watched as the car left the driveway with a huge sigh of relief. Kessen reinstated Izzy into the pack, and Izzy had her friendship with Brightie renewed. The peaceful atmosphere of the sorority house was once again restored, and in a strange way, they owed it all to Tansy.

Kessen not only restored Izzy's position but also gave her a special plastic disc to practice her jumping. If Izzy wanted to be a champion athlete, Kessen would support her as long as she gave equal time to assistance work during her training months. Izzy's dreams were finally coming true, but often dreams turned to nightmares.

Because of a family crisis, Tansy's foster family weren't able to keep Tansy, and our folks offered to take her and include her in the training program for assistance. After only two weeks of peace and quiet, Tansy was returning to the sorority house and not just for a visit. Their lives would unquestionably change in ways not even imaginable. But, Kessen put their minds at ease when he put Tansy's return into perspective. He reminded them that since they had survived Izzy's tornado-like arrival, Tansy's transition to the household would be an easy situation in comparison. Although Izzy was a bit offended by the reminder, Brightie felt a lot better about the changes that were about to occur in their living situation.

Tansy arrived and was confident that she would make a new start in this household. She admitted to herself that she had missed the company of the other dogs and especially Izzy's mentoring. She might not have many opportunities for life as a *party girl*, but at least she'd be with friends. After appropriate greetings and, of course, a review of the rules by Kessen, Tansy followed Izzy and Brightie out into the yard. When she passed the toy basket with Kessen's ring toy sticking out, she didn't even take a second look. She just walked on by and avoided any temptation. She remembered getting the *stink-eye* from Kessen and didn't want a repeat of that scary occurrence. The dogs played nicely, and after a while, even Tansy needed a nap. Izzy and Brightie were really surprised since they rarely saw Tansy sleep during her first visit to the sorority house. Perhaps, Tansy's stay with them wouldn't be as difficult as they thought.

Tansy's training began the next day, and she spent short periods of time during the day learning her name, taking treats gently from our mom's hands and practicing her Sit command. Training was very new to her, but after the sessions, she was allowed to play with Brightie and Izzy. Kessen remained in the background in a supervisory capacity and only intervened if their play became too rowdy. Between training sessions and playing in the yard, the days just flew by. Tansy was enrolled in obedience classes and was excited about everything that

Training came before play time.

she did. Her energy was endless and often proved exhausting for the other dogs. Tansy was busy doing something almost every minute of the day. When she became overly energetic, our mom had her stay in the kitchen behind the gate for a while. What was meant as a calming technique wasn't very effective. The time-out merely served as a means of renewing her energy.

Although Brightie lived vicariously through Izzy's escapades and thoroughly enjoyed hearing about her public outings, she also made time during her day for Tansy. The two of them developed a most unusual friendship in that Brightie was low-keyed, and Tansy's energy level was off the charts. When Tansy was confined to the kitchen to curb her enthusiasm, Brightie would often lay on the throw rug beside the gate to keep her company. Tansy would then lean through the bars of the gate and clean Brightie ears by licking them. Brightie would move her head from side to side so Tansy would give each ear a good cleaning. Leave it to Brightie to get Tansy to groom her. Brightie's ability to get things done for her amazed Kessen and Izzy, and all it took was her innocent-looking face, eyes the color of dark chocolate and curly eyelashes.

When Izzy went off to advanced training, the bond between Tansy and Brightie grew. Tansy's training accelerated as new commands were readily introduced. Because of Tansy's energetic behavior, our mom worked with her in the kitchen area. Brightie remained on the other side of the gate and would mimic

Their friendship grew.

the commands given to Tansy. Brightie already knew all of the commands, so she was destined for treats. Our mom, not wanting to short change Brightie, often gave her a small bit of kibble for her response to the commands as well. It was a win-win situation for both dogs.

Tansy was also a bit of a prankster and enjoyed playing games with the dogs. She didn't like to mess around with Kessen but never hesitated playing a practical joke on Brightie. One day, Brightie had some sort of procedure done at the animal hospital and came home wearing a huge cone on her head. Brightie was not at all pleased with her appearance since her looks meant everything to her, and the color of the cone did nothing for her complexion. In addition to the humiliation, the cone originally belonged to Kessen, and the folks thought it unnecessary to purchase another one when Kessen's would work just fine. Tansy heard the folks say that the cone had something called Velcro panels on it to make it adjustable. Tansy didn't know what that was, but that sticky stuff kept the cone on Brightie's head. However, Brightie's neck was quite a bit smaller than Kessen's. Because of that, the cone around her neck was very loose, and two panels of the sticky stuff were exposed. Tansy saw this as a perfect opportunity to play a trick on Brightie and hopefully make her laugh. Brightie was much too sensitive about her looks and needed to know that she didn't look all that funny while wearing it.

For the trick to work, Tansy needed to entice Brightie into playing a game they had devised during their training sessions. Since Brightie often mimicked the commands as Tansy did them, the two of them challenged each other to see who could do the commands the fastest. They'd go through various commands, judge who did them the fastest and had a lot of fun along the way. The game really didn't make much sense, but it was great source of amusement on rainy days when they couldn't play out in the yard.

Tansy, the instigator of practical jokes, was now ready to take Brightie's mind off the cone by playing their game

Brightie was stuck!

together. Tansy was on one throw rug, and Brightie was on another. Tansy did a few Sits and Stands in quick succession while Brightie continued to mimic her. Even with that enormous cone flapping on her head, Brightie followed Tansy's demonstration of commands. The excitement levels intensified as the dogs moved swiftly through their motions which made the game even more fun for both of them. Until now, Tansy had refrained from doing the Down command but was now ready for its use. As if the command were given, she dropped to the floor and assumed the Down position. Brightie, following Tansy's lead, did the same but had forgotten that she was wearing the cone with the sticky panels exposed. As a result, Brightie was now stuck to the throw rug and wasn't quite sure what to do. Because her entire body was on the rug, she couldn't even stand up because the rug was attached to the cone. Tansy rolled around the floor in a fit of howling and barking that brought the folks running to the kitchen. They spotted Brightie in a perfect Down position but, regrettably, stuck to the rug. They knew immediately that Tansy was somehow responsible for this strange situation because she quickly disappeared into her kennel and pretended to be asleep. They freed Brightie from the throw rug and, as a reward for tolerating Tansy's naughtiness, gave her a special frozen treat made especially for dogs. Needless to say, Tansy didn't get anything, and Brightie declared that the joke was on her.

Tansy enjoyed life and appreciated everything and everyone around her. She had such a cheerful look about her as if she were smiling all of the time. Even if she were being disciplined for running around the house with a shoe or shredding a fallen bill from the desk, she gave the appearance of smiling. The folks thought that Tansy showed no remorse about anything that she did, and surprisingly, that characteristic was charming to them. Human judgement was, at times, very confusing for the canines of the sorority house.

Somewhere along the way, she was given the nicknames of Wiggle-Butt and T-T-Pinquay. Now, she knew that the nickname of Wiggle-Butt resulted from her continuous rear-end movement and wagging tail but didn't have a clue as to what T-T-Pinquay had to do with anything. One day, that name just popped out of our mom's mouth, and it seemed to stick. Tansy, being somewhat confused by this whole business of giving nicknames, asked Izzy about it while they were resting after some

Strange Nickname

yard play. Izzy admitted that she was just as confused about the nicknames because sometimes they made sense and other times, they did not. For example, when she first arrived at the sorority house, she took the house by storm and her nicknames ranged from the Dust Demon to the most offensive...the Izz-Manian Devil. Now, in truth, she deserved each of those names. However, as her behavior improved, the nickname changed. Before long, she was called Izz-Whykal by family members. Izzy didn't have a clue as to what led to that nickname, but that's what our mom called her once, and the rest was history. Because she thought her neighbor named Finnegan was a roustabout and a goofball, she didn't count the nicknames of Toots and Honey that he gave her. Anyway, Izzy went on to explain that some of the dogs had reasonable nicknames...Kessen was K-Man, Brightie was Brightie Girl or Sweet Cheeks, Marnie was Marnie Girl and Turin was T-Man. Those names made sense, but Izz-Whykal and T-T-Pinquay were off the charts of common sense and not even indicative of any sort of behavior. Izzy felt that it was all too baffling and probably not worth the time to figure it out. For the first time ever, Tansy agreed with Izzy's assessment which just proved that anything was possible.

Since the dogs were addressing the puzzling elements of their lives, Tansy asked how their house got the name of sorority house. Izzy said that it was quite a reasonable name given the circumstances. Kessen was actually the one who came up with the name, but it wasn't intentional that it be permanent. Turin had already gone on to advanced training, and Kessen declared himself to be the ruling male of the household. Izzy sort of chuckled at his declaration because, at the time, Kessen was the only dog in residence. He had no competition whatsoever for the ruling position, but Brightie wasn't about to bring that to his attention. Then, Brightie came along, and the two of them formed the pack...more like a twosome, but Kessen insisted it was a pack, and he, of course, claimed leadership. Brightie was fine with this decision since she wasn't one who enjoyed any type of responsibility. Then, along came Marnie...another female entered the house. Kessen was beside himself and wondered why the folks weren't bringing another male dog into the house. These females were driving him to gulp water instead of just drink slowly, and that caused problems with his digestive system.

One day when his frustration level was at its peak with the female bickering, Kessen announced that he wasn't in charge of a pack of dogs in the house, but, instead, responsible for mediating problems in a house full of females. He went on to claim that it wasn't just a house...it was more like a sorority house! Brightie and Marnie looked at each other and burst into howling over Kessen's proclamation. According to them, this was the perfect name for the house, and they would call it that from now on. Kessen shook his head in frustration, refused to engage in their silliness and walked away. Sometimes, he just couldn't win with the females of the pack.

Tansy was happy that she and Izzy were finally friends, but soon, Izzy went off to advanced training for assistance work. When she first came to the sorority house, Izzy was determined to be a champion athlete, but sometime during her training for assistance, her dream changed. She was born to help others, and advanced training was just the way to make this happen. The entire family was pleased with her decision, but it meant that they probably wouldn't ever see her again. In his ultimate wisdom as the pack leader, Kessen reminded them that Izzy's friendship remained in their hearts and her memories in their minds. Brightie and Tansy had to give Kessen credit…he always knew the right thing to say.

Now, Kessen, Brightie and Tansy formed the new pack. Kessen and Brightie were involved in assisted therapy work, and Tansy continued her training for assistance. She really enjoyed being in public, but then Tansy enjoyed everything. She attended the weekly church service and liked listening to the music. Once in a while, she'd attempt to gnaw on a book in the section under the seat in front of her, but a swift snap of the leash stopped that behavior. Sometimes, she'd even try to

scratch the grout from lines in the tiled floor, but she was immediately stopped with a quick correction. The folks had eyes everywhere and never allowed her to get away with anything. So, Tansy decided to just relax and enjoy the service.

She had to behave in church.

Brightie warned her not to give in to the temptation of drinking from the Holy Water Fountain that was located by the exit door. Kessen tried it as a puppy and was abruptly stopped with a gentle leash correction. Izzy thought about doing it many times but didn't risk getting caught. Tansy passed the Holy Water Fountain every Sunday as they left the church but heeded Brightie's explicit warning. It was, however, quite the temptation.

Then, the fun really began with a trip across the street to the bagel store. That was Tansy's favorite place to visit since the aromas of fresh bagels and pastries filled the air and tickled her nostrils in a most pleasing way. The folks took Tansy there regularly and sat next to the carry-out section. It was the perfect location for her to see the people coming in, deciding on their choices of pastries at the counter and then either staying for their meal or taking it home. Often, people stopped at their table and asked to pet her. They were permitted to do so but only if Tansy remained seated. Tansy didn't see the sense to this, but it was the only way she would get that type of attention. Even the staff members practiced greetings with Tansy when they had free time, and she truly enjoyed the attention.

The folks took Tansy to other places while she was in training, and not all of the experiences were positive ones. Tansy had so much energy that the folks would often have to have her run around the yard to burn off that extra energy before going out in public. Going to an indoor mall to meet a group of dogs in training was a total disaster for Tansy. Struggling to gain traction on the slippery floors and attempting to pass dogs of all ages without lunging, was just too over-stimulating for Tansy. As a result, she just seemed to shut down from the exertion of controlling herself in this atmosphere. The folks took Tansy home and allowed her to rest for a while. They would visit the mall again when there weren't as many distractions. Everyone in the household noticed this was the only time that Tansy wasn't smiling as well as one of the few times that she slept.

What Tansy did best was to bounce back from disappointment, and as usual, she accomplished this with such enthusiasm. A week later, her next visit to the mall was quite different, and she was relaxed the entire time. Even the music from a brass band playing for a group of school children didn't faze her. Wiggle Butt was back in stride, and her ever popular smile was back again.

Tansy was quite a rascal and often got herself into trouble. Sometimes, her actions were quite serious and even, at times, dangerous. Because she had this uncanny knowledge of when regular hospital hours ended and emergency fees began, she became a frequent visitor to the veterinary hospital's emergency room. Tansy was, first and foremost, a silent shredder. In total silence, she'd take something and shred it to bits in the blink of an eye. She managed this because whatever she shredded was usually something that she never bothered with in the past. She might play with a squeak toy for weeks, and then one day shred it to bits. While crated in the back of the car on a road trip, she had secretly eaten half of a pillow case that covered her bed. The pillow case had gone untouched for months until that day. When the folks reached their destination in the evening, they discovered what she had done. They weren't sure if she had shredded it before swallowing it or had torn sections off and eaten them. Swallowing things whole spelled disaster to her intestinal tract. Upon advice of their veterinarian, the folks took her to the emergency room for an x-ray of her stomach. Fortunately, there appeared to be no obstruction, and true to form, Tansy had shredded the material, eaten it in small pieces that were no threat to her stomach.

Tansy's Fun

Tansy loved to carry things around the house and was often seen with a toy or a bone in her mouth. Sometimes, she'd even grab a tablespoon that dropped from the table and walk around. Some dogs don't like to retrieve metal items and someday, as a helper dog, she might be required to pick up these types of objects. Consequently, nothing was done to discourage this behavior. One evening, Tansy watched as our mom transferred clothes from the washing machine to the dryer. As the clothes were moved, coins that were somehow left in the pockets flew all over the room. Our mom immediately gave Tansy the Out command which instructed her to leave the room and sit by the threshold. Quickly glancing at Tansy, our mom saw Tansy make a swallowing gesture with her mouth. Swallowed coins were extremely dangerous to a dog's well-being. After calling the veterinarian, our mom was instructed to take Tansy in once again for an x-ray. Of course, it was well after regular hospital hours, so it was another visit to the emergency room. Fortunately, the x-ray was clear, and Tansy hadn't picked up any of the coins. While our mom kept telling herself that the trip wasn't a wasted endeavor because it was better to be safe than sorry, Tansy regarded that trip as just another opportunity to see her favorite veterinarian. However, from that night on, all canines were banned from the laundry room.

While it might seem that Tansy was unsupervised, this wasn't the case at all. She was not only a silent shredder but was also an accomplished thief. She didn't regard her actions as really stealing, but merely a means of moving things from one place to another. She took great pride in her phantom-like ability to remove some object in the blink of an eye without any sudden detection from the folks. After a while, Tansy gave up the pretense and brazenly engaged in this type of behavior right in front of the family. She'd be sitting nicely around the kitchen counter and with the speed of a flea jumping onto an

unprotected dog, Tansy would grab an orange from the fruit bowl and then run around the house with it in her mouth. She wanted the folks to chase her, but they didn't play that game. Even Kessen and Brightie knew better than to engage in this type of behavior. Once Tansy realized

The Phantom Thief

that she wasn't going to be chased, she eventually returned to the scene of the crime and dropped the orange on the floor. This happened with everything that Tansy seized or, as she referred to it, gently removed from its original place. She just seemed to enjoy the excitement of the theft and always returned the item in good condition.

Eventually, the folks removed all small objects from the end tables and kept the fruit bowl where Tansy couldn't possibly reach it. In an effort to correct the misbehavior, the folks set a trap for Tansy. A cookie sheet was positioned on the edge of the kitchen counter with table spoons on top and a special treat in the middle. According to the plan, when Tansy reached up to get the treat from the cookie sheet, the sheet would fall, and the noise created by the spoons falling to the floor would act as a deterrent for future thievery. Now, Kessen and Brightie, who had both foolishly fallen prey to that cookie sheet caper when they were young, knew from first-paw experience that it definitely worked…most of the time. They watched in anticipation of Tansy's surprise, but when she reached for the treat and the cookie sheet fell with the spoons rattling, it didn't bother her a bit. She not only took the treat, but also ran around with one of the tablespoons in her mouth that fell to the floor. The folks just shook their heads in amazement while Kessen and Brightie wondered why it had worked on them. Tansy was, indeed, a force to be reckoned with at every turn of events.

While Tansy enjoyed mischievous behavior, she had so many good qualities that made her extra-special. What people noticed first of all was her enjoyment of life. Even the folks mentioned that she was the happiest dog they had ever trained. She was an enthusiastic learner, enjoyed being around people, played well with other dogs and had learned all of her commands in a short period of time. While she earned the nickname of Wiggle-Butt, there were some quiet moments for her. The folks had purchased a lounge chair especially made for dogs and positioned it by the bay window in the dining room. It was initially meant as a training device since the dogs in training had to learn to get on and off various types of furniture on command. Tansy did well going up and down ramps positioned at all heights, so the folks figured that this would be just as easy for her. Before the command of On was out of our mom's mouth, Tansy was sitting comfortably on that lounge chair.

She loved her lounge chair.

During the day when not training in public, she'd lay on that lounge chair for lengthy periods of time. She watched the children playing next door, dogs chasing each other, squirrels and chipmunks climbing up and down the tree in the garden and the people passing on the sidewalk. She never once thought to bark at anything or anyone that passed by. Being on that lounge chair was just her special place, and surprisingly, neither Kessen nor Brightie ever jumped on that chair because they recognized it belonged to Tansy.

Tansy's training time at the sorority house was coming to an end. During her final week, the folks took her to say good bye to the friends that she had met during her training. It was a sad time for the folks as well as for Kessen and Brightie. In spite of her naughtiness and rambunctious behavior, everyone would miss Tansy's smiling face and the happiness that she brought to the sorority house. As they had done with all of the dogs before sending them off to advanced training, the folks took Tansy to church for the last time and had her blessed by their favorite priest. He truly loved dogs, and after the service and the blessing, he played with Tansy for a while. That event signaled the

Tansy's Special Blessing

ending of Tansy's stay in the sorority house but was just the beginning of the next exciting chapter in her life.

The next day, the entire family traveled to the training facility to say their good byes to Tansy and wish her well on her journey. While it was definitely a sad time for the family, Tansy was on her way to new and exciting experiences that would shape her life, and everyone knew how much Tansy loved excitement. The family would always remember her as the rambunctious dog who remained a puppy in spirit and had a heart of gold.

Well, that was Kessen's version of my story, and if I had told the story from my point of view, I might have focused more on my good qualities and less on my high-spirited behavior. Little did the family know that years later, when my retirement from service came about, they would accept me back into the sorority house as a permanent resident. They were unquestionably gluttons for punishment, but my years of service had changed me for the better. Kessen and Brightie enthusiastically welcomed me back, and Kessen even offered to teach me the art of storytelling. How wonderful is that? Of course, I still enjoy a bit of naughtiness now and then, but life without some mischief is a life without adventure…

Life is meant to be enjoyed!

Harley

Since the folks left in such a rush with Kessen early this morning, they forgot to turn on the television or even leave a light on for us. It is very late, and without much light in the sunroom, it is getting difficult to see the Wall of Fame. Brightie walks around the house, looks out of the windows and periodically hovers around her food bowl. Our internal stomach clocks signal that dinner time had already come and gone, but staring at the food bowl isn't going to make the dinner appear. Within the last hour, I have gone from out and out worry to downright panic over not knowing what is happening with Kessen. I know that panicking wouldn't change anything, but I am not sure what else to do.

I still have one more story to share and just enough light to see this last picture clearly. Since I was already living at the sorority house when this seventh puppy arrived, I have decided to deviate a bit from Kessen's version and take the risk of telling it from my own personal experiences. It might not be as good as Kessen's version, but one has to take some risks in life. Since I might eventually take over the task of storytelling, I'd better just jump in and get my paws wet with this last puppy's story.

The seventh dog, who entered the sorority house, was an energetic, black Labrador Retriever named Harley. His situation was different than ours in the sense that he spent time with two families. His foster family, whose jobs required that they travel occasionally, asked if Harley might stay with us at the sorority house when they were out of town. Our folks were happy to help them and even offered to get Harley from the training facility. This great arrangement gave Harley a variety of experiences with two families, and at the same time, gave each family a bit of a break when Harley wasn't with them. After spending time with Harley, everyone, both canine and human, needed some time off.

The folks knew about the arrangement for about six weeks before getting Harley. During that time period, they diligently prepared for his arrival. They made changes gradually so resident pack members wouldn't blame Harley for any disruption in their daily routines. The folks hoped for a smooth transition to the changes in the living arrangements for all of the dogs...including Harley. One day, the gates appeared in the kitchen and in the hallway. Soon, smaller dog kennels were positioned in various rooms, and smaller food and water bowls occupied the space next to the kitchen kennel. A basket of small toys appeared on the opposite side of the kitchen kennel, and our food bowls were moved to another location.

Once the area rugs were rolled up and stored, we knew that our days of peaceful solitude were rapidly coming to an end.

The folks thought that they were fooling us by doing these things gradually, but we knew what was happening. Kessen didn't mind the inconvenience of walking through an opening in a gate to get to the kitchen, and I certainly didn't mind the area rugs being gone. But, Brightie, the resident diva, thought that walking ten extra feet to reach her food bowl was the height of inconvenience. Kessen just gave a sigh and, in an effort to avoid another conflict, sauntered to another room in the house. Since I enjoyed a bit of teasing, I suggested that perhaps Brightie might get this new arrival to bring food to her rather than having her walk the extra distance to her food bowls. She immediately recognized my sarcasm and wasn't at all amused. Sometimes Brightie Girl or Sweet Cheeks, as she was called, had no sense of humor...especially when it came to work.

We also knew that when the time came for getting this new puppy, we'd be invited along for the ride. Our being in the car was supposed to make the puppy feel at home from the start, but we knew that our presence was meant to curtail the puppy's howling on the way home. Sure, we were dogs and not expected to be wise to the ways of the world, but we sniffed out that ulterior motive as soon as they told us we were going for a car ride.

When that day came, we knew that this was the day of Harley's arrival. As planned, Kessen, Brightie and I were invited to go along for the ride to the facility. When the door to the backseat of the car was opened, I sidestepped protocol, jumped into the backseat and positioned myself on the right side of the car. Once again, Kessen sat in the middle of the backseat so he could look out the front window, and Brightie positioned herself on the left. Because she was second in the pack, she was supposed to choose her seating before I did and not having that opportunity angered her. Before she could confront me regarding my rudeness, the car started moving. Once this happened, we weren't allowed to move around in the vehicle. Instead, we either had to remain in a sitting or down position. No jaw sparing or air snapping was allowed while the car was in motion. This sound advice prevented Brightie from demanding an explanation of my actions. Kessen remained neutral so as not to be involved in the female bickering that occurred on a daily basis.

While each of us slept most of the way to the training facility, we quickly awakened when the car reached its destination. Everyone was anxious to meet the new puppy. We already knew that the puppy was an eight week old, male, black Labrador Retriever named Harley and hoped that he'd enjoy staying with us at the sorority house. Needless to say, Kessen was overjoyed at the prospect of having another male dog in the house. The pack would finally be gender-balanced, and Harley's presence might even curtail some of the squabbling that occurred every day.

We also understood that Harley wouldn't be with us all of the time since the folks were co-raising him with another family, but everyone would certainly enjoy having him around when he did stay with us. With Harley's arrival, Brightie had one more member of the pack to do her bidding...even if it meant having him for short periods of time. According to Brightie, additional help was still help and always greatly appreciated for any length of time.

When our mom came out of the training center with Harley, the first thing that the we noticed was his distinctive Labrador Retriever characteristics. The shape of his head in

relation to his body was indicative of a superior genetic background. While his coat was fluffy and shiny, his ears had somewhat of a velvety texture to them. This dog was going to grow up to be quite a good looking dog. Then, we saw his paws...beautifully shaped but the size of hamburger patties. When he grew into those paws,

Great Looking Pup

Harley was going to be a huge, handsome dog!

I was a bit disillusioned when our mom allowed Harley to ride in the front seat with her for the ride home. I thought that I was the only one who shared this experience when first coming to the sorority house. Now, I learned from Kessen that most of the puppies had the same opportunity. My reasons for self-importance were dwindling slightly with every passing mile.

Brightie, reverting to her role of co-captain of the Socialization Squad, acknowledged that Harley was a real looker in the canine sense, but reminded me that as a pack member, I also had the responsibility of demonstrating proper social skills and encouraging public etiquette at all times. This meant no excessive fooling around, limited enthusiastic play and absolutely no engaging in mischievous behavior when Harley was at the house. These stipulations covered a hefty part of his upbringing and would take a strong paw to keep him in line. In her opinion, good looks only went so far in this life. Who was she kidding? Her innocent looks and curly eyelashes earned her just about everything that she had, and all I had to rely on were my wits and wisdom to get ahead. While hearing what I just said, I realized that Brightie had a lot more going for her than I did. So consequently, I would work hard with Harley, and we would make a perfect match as minions of the pack.

Harley seemed quite compliant when the folks picked him up from the facility. He slept a good portion of the time in our mom's lap on the ride home and never offered any resistance to being held which was a very good sign in terms of his temperament. Kessen, as co-captain of the Socialization Squad, had to start with the basics in terms of puppy behavior, and my guess was that he'd start with a lecture that included Harley's first face-to-face encounter with the dreaded *stink-eye*.

Once we got home, Kessen, Brightie and I jumped out of the backseat, and our mom put Harley down on the grass. He really seemed to enjoy the feel of it since he began rolling around on his back. At such an early age, this pup knew how to have a good time. When I was younger, I enjoyed the feel of the grass on my back, but Brightie claimed that she never engaged in that sort of behavior because it would mess up her flaxen coat. She was a real diva and wouldn't even go outside when there was moisture on the deck because she didn't like getting the pads of her paws wet. I sensed that Harley was in for some etiquette lessons when Brightie took over his mentoring.

After proper greetings, Kessen gave his welcome lecture complete with the scary *stink-eye*. Brightie and I watched as Harley actually listened attentively to Kessen's rules and regulations, and we were amazed that Harley actually paid attention to him. Maybe he was mesmerized by the *stink-eye* or maybe it was just the beginnings of male bonding. We could see that he had already found favor with Kessen by paying total attention to his lecture. We'll see what happens once Harley gets accustomed to being here because that's when the true puppy emerges and trouble begins. We refer to the puppy's first few days of good behavior

Harley actually listened to Kessen.

as the honeymoon period. When this phase ends, the true puppy antics start, and our jobs begin.

Harley had great respect for Kessen as the pack leader and never used his sharp, puppy teeth on him. Instead, he saved that behavior for us. He loved to play but, as a puppy, didn't really know the rules regarding soft mouthing. Our job was to set him straight. It was time for Linus' Three Step Action Plan. Brightie actually learned that method from Linus himself when he stayed at the house for a week of

He loved to wrestle.

socialization many years ago. My first encounter with this plan was when I came to visit for a weekend, and a dog in training named Izzy used it on me. It was truly an effective teaching technique using a combination of a curled lip, low growl and muffled snap. After using this technique a few times on Harley, he eventually got the message. Even though he was a rough player, once Harley turned his attention to squeak toys, ropes and balls, his attacks on us weren't as frequent. Brightie and I secretly hoped for the days when Harley would start losing his sharp, baby teeth. Only then would we be totally safe from his rambunctious behavior, and our days of doubling as his pin cushions would end.

The folks had their responsibilities, as well, in terms of Harley's behavior. Judging from the size of Harley's paws, the folks had better have a solid foundation for proper leash behavior and public etiquette from the get-go. Without the proper guidance and consistency in these areas, Harley would have a field day dragging the folks around the neighborhood. I had to admit that each time Harley visited us, the sorority house was turned into an amusement park complete with the ups and downs of a roller coaster ride. Adventure lurked around every corner of each room in the house.

Harley loved adventure!

Harley only stayed with us for short periods of time, and just when we thought he was getting into the routine of being here, his foster family took him to their house. While we were a bit sad to see him go, we were going to enjoy the serenity of the household while we could. Kessen, thinking that he'd inject a bit of humor into the moment, reminded us that someday when Harley returned, he'd have a full set of adult teeth. Both Brightie and I decided right then and there that we each needed to find a good hiding place for his future visits.

Harley came to stay with us for a weekend a few weeks later, but it turned out to be a quiet one for him. On the way to our house, he silently ripped open a paper bag of doughnut holes that had mistakenly fallen out of the shopping bag in the back seat of the car. By the time he got to our house, Harley had consumed the entire contents of the bag. What surprised me was the fact that he didn't eat the bag as well.

He was one sick puppy for the weekend and wasn't feeling up to playing with us. The folks kept him in the

sunroom by himself near the dog run in case he had to make a quick exit. His meals consisted of poached chicken and rice to get his digestive system back on track. He was feeling fine by Sunday when his foster family came to pick him up, but I can't say that he had a great time with us. We, on the other paw, had one of the few quiet weekends with Harley.

Rough Weekend

A few months passed before we saw Harley again. But, when he returned for a brief stay with us, he had drastically changed. He was much larger, weighed a great deal more and had grown into those large paws of his. Just as Kessen predicted, Harley had a full set of bright, white teeth that contrasted greatly with his coal-black coat. He walked with a certain elegance that made his appearance quite stunning. Brightie and I both did double takes when we first saw him. As Brightie so elegantly put it...Harley was a real hunk!

Harley enjoyed playing in the yard and was quite the athlete. Once in a while, the folks would put up the agility equipment and have mock competitions with us. Kessen always assumed his supervisory position on the pause table, while Brightie, Harley and I went through the course with each of the folks. Brightie blasted through the tunnels at top speed while I specialized in going through the weave poles. Harley was good at everything…especially going over the hurdles. That dog soared over each one easily and never knocked a bar from its stationary position. Brightie and I thought that he could probably jump over our fence if he tried, but we didn't mention this to him because our folks would punish us forever if we encouraged that sort of behavior. After all, we were supposed to be good examples for Harley.

Harley was special.

Because Harley wasn't with us too often, he didn't get to do all of the things with our folks that they typically did with a dog in training. They did, however, take him to restaurants, shopping centers, their favorite bagel shop as well as the weekly church service. The other training experiences were left to his main foster family. All in all, Harley was quite the traveler as he adjusted to each residence easily.

It was time for Harley to go into advanced training, and since his foster family had to be out of town for the weekend, they asked our folks if they might take him back to the facility. Harley had been staying with us for a while anyway, so it was an easy transition. The folks were happy to oblige since Harley was such a wonderful dog and was, in many ways, a member of the family. As an additional surprise, the folks were also going to bring back a service dog for an individual in the area who wasn't able to pick the dog up himself. Our folks believed there was always room for one more dog in the car or in the house.

On the day that Harley was to go back, we all piled into the back seat of the car. After a bit of commotion regarding sitting positions, we were finally ready for the ride to the facility. While sharing this last car ride with Harley, we looked back on our times spent with him and realized how he resembled each of the sorority house dogs in terms of behavior. To begin with, Harley was quite

Jumper

the jumper...much like Turin who was the first dog who entered the sorority house. Harley was similar to Kessen in terms of his leadership skills but also demonstrated quite a sensitive side when another dog

Leader

needed a much softer approach. His dignified and dapper appearance reminded us of Brightie's attempts at appearing well-groomed at all times, and his running around the yard at top speed with his body close to the ground totally duplicated Izzy's memorable, tornado-

Charmer

like behavior. In the evening, Harley would often sit by our mom's favorite recliner as she read the evening newspaper just like Marnie used to do, and he just loved relaxing on my lounge chair located in the bay window while he watched the children playing in the

Athlete

yard next door. His love of adventure was

Helper

even similar to my nature. Recognizing that Harley resembled each of the dogs who shared time at the sorority house was quite an awesome realization, yet we never noticed it until now.

Harley, being Harley, just took the similarities in stride. He was just happy to have shared his early months with such wonderful dogs. Now, having been told that he resembled them in various ways was

Rascal

an added bonus. While Harley would definitely miss us, he would always keep our memories close to his heart.

Harley was, undeniably, our Weekend Warrior, but in the end, he left us with quite a wonderful gift. Because of the shared similarities with each of the dogs, he was, in a sense, taking a bit of each of us with him on his journey toward assistance. While time spent with Harley in the sorority house was very much like a continuous roller coaster ride, we never imagined that he would inadvertently take us all along for the ride in advanced training...

Harley represented the best in all of us.

PART III
EVENING

It is very dark in the house now and watching Brightie walking back and forth in front of her food bowls makes me so uneasy. In an effort to take her mind off her food, which is one extremely difficult task, I ask her to join me in the laundry room to wait for the folks and Kessen to return. At least we'd be closer to hearing the garage door opening from that vantage point when they did come home. I didn't want my sense of urgency to show, but I knew that dogs were very perceptive. Even if she were engrossed in food-bowl stalking, she would

They're finally home!

spot my heightened apprehension easily. I didn't know how to hide that from her.

As I was about to mention something to her, I heard the creaking of the garage door as it slowly opened. The folks were finally coming home, and everything would be all right. That was my hope, but deep down in my heart, I knew that our lives would never be the same. They were gone from the house for much too long of a period of time for things to be okay.

It seemed to take forever for the folks to open the door, but when they did, Kessen was the first to enter. He usually had such a spirited gait, but this evening, his entrance was slow as he cautiously crossed the tiled floor. Somehow, Brightie and I knew enough not to welcome him in our usual enthusiastic manner. He appeared to have gone through a tough day, and we certainly didn't want to make it worse for him.

The folks immediately turned on the lights and noticed that we were loose in the house all day long. However, instead of checking all of rooms for turmoil or destruction, they never mentioned anything about it. They were so preoccupied with Kessen that they didn't even notice the multitude of blonde, dog hairs on both the couch and the loveseat. This was just another example of Brightie's having good luck. Apparently, staying in my kennel and behaving appropriately was a wasted opportunity for sleeping on the furniture. At least, I had the satisfaction of knowing that I did the right thing when faced with a crisis…that was my only justification for missing out on some couch comfort.

As my eyes adjusted to the lights in the house, I saw that Kessen had a huge ring toy around his neck. It wasn't his special toy because I made sure that was kept safe for him, but instead, it was puffy and above all, very clean. I wondered why he was wearing this cumbersome ring toy around his neck. Kessen wasn't accustomed to making any sort of fashion statements, so there must be a specific reason for his wearing it. Then, I saw the bandage around his stomach and immediately knew that he had some type of operation, and what he had around his neck wasn't a ring toy at all. Whatever it was called, it kept him from removing his bandage. Seeing him like that raised my concern. Brightie had even left her sentry duty around her food bowl to see what had happened.

The folks noticed our concern and told us that Kessen had to have a small operation, but that he'd be fine in a day or two. We weren't supposed to bother him at all because he needed his rest. I immediately felt relieved, was sorry that I wasted the entire day worrying about him and especially regretted not sleeping on the furniture. Both Brightie and I were so relieved to see that Kessen really looked fine and was happy to see us. He just needed some rest after such a hectic day.

Kessen needed peace and quiet.

Our mom, noticing that we had been left alone for the entire day without the benefit of lights or the television being on as a distraction, told us how very proud that she was of our behavior…especially since we weren't even in our kennels. As a reward for being so trustworthy, not only would we get our dinner, but we would also get a special frozen treat meant especially for dogs. It was a great reward for our good behavior.

We weren't allowed to play with Kessen after eating, but he looked okay after having rested for a while. He told us that he was happy to be home and actually missed us during his somewhat stressful day at the animal hospital. Kessen wondered how we'd behave on our own because he saw that the folks didn't do the typical things before leaving the house like kenneling us, putting the television on and leaving a light on for us. He actually expected to find evidence of our being on the furniture when he returned. Hopefully, he wouldn't notice the blonde, dog hair on the couch and loveseat on his way to the dog run. If he did, the *stink-eye* wouldn't be far behind and would definitely be directed at us. But, fate was once again on Brightie's side because the folks fenced off an area in the living room giving Kessen easier access to the dog run. Brightie was saved from any reprimand since Kessen wouldn't pass the furniture by using that other door. They also included Kessen's bed in the enclosure with a clean, white sheet over it so he'd have something fresh to sleep on later in the evening. We decided to sleep next to him on the other side of the fenced area so he'd have company if he woke up during the night and wanted to talk.

As I watched Kessen sleeping so soundly with that ring around his neck, I thought about how Brightie and I had spent our entire day while waiting for everyone to return. In the morning, we walked around the house looking for mischief and decided against it. Brightie spent the afternoon sleeping on forbidden furniture. I, on the other paw, occupied my time by progressing through various levels of apprehension beginning with concern and ending up with out and out panic regarding Kessen's situation. However, on the plus side, sharing Kessen's stories from the pictures on the Wall of Fame made the time pass quickly and gave me confidence in my ability to share his stories. Perhaps someday, under Kessen's guidance, I'll be able to follow in his paw-steps as another storyteller in the household. I can't wait to tell him all about my experiences tomorrow when he wakes up.

Since Kessen needs his rest following his procedure, Brightie and I will probably be responsible for the majority of the work during the next few weeks. The holidays are quickly approaching, and Harley will be spending some time with us as soon as Kessen is up and around. Since Harley is a bit of a rambunctious puppy, he won't visit until Kessen is well-healed. Knowing Harley's fascination with leaping over all sorts of enclosures, he'd be in Kessen's fenced area before anyone blinked an eye. This, in itself, would be disastrous.

As I relive the events of today in my mind before going to sleep, I must admit that this day was probably the most stressful and, at the same time, the most fulfilling day since my return to the sorority house following my retirement from service. Getting re-acquainted with all of the dogs from the Wall of Fame by sharing their stories gave me such a sense of accomplishment and pride in having been a part of it all. Training puppies to help others is a wonderful experience to pass on to future puppies, and having Kessen and Brightie share this extraordinary way of life with me is such a wonderful blessing.

Waiting for Kessen and the folks to return from the animal hospital was definitely a thought provoking experience. I learned a lot about myself as well as what I need to do in the future to assist other puppies who come to this special place. It was a magical experience because these wonderful dogs as mentors changed lives, created dreams and shaped futures. They did it all in the hopes of helping others...

Today was a learning experience.

CONCLUSION

This coming Christmas would be our first holiday without Kessen. Two weeks ago during our first snowstorm, he and the folks went for a car ride, and they returned without him. They looked like they had been crying, but we weren't sure of the reason. A few days before their trip, Kessen mentioned that he was considering retirement from being the pack leader and might be leaving us for a place called the Rainbow Bridge. He assured us that if and when he went there, he'd be with a lot of retired pack leaders, and they'd all have a great time together. There would be no rules for the pack leaders to enforce, complete access to treats and days filled with fun, rest and relaxation. It sounded like an all-inclusive canine resort to me. I remembered telling Kessen that it just might be a great place to visit, but he told me not to rush to get there. Since pack leaders had a tendency to stick together, they probably just wanted the place all to themselves. I totally understood his need for some peace and quiet.

Between Brightie's constant bickering, Harley's raucous behavior and Kessen's teaching me the art of storytelling, he really needed a break from us. He also told us that if he decided to retire, Brightie, being next in line, would become the new pack leader. Between the possibility of his leaving and the opportunity of Brightie's rise to power, I didn't know which of the two posed the greatest threat. Without any deliberation whatsoever, the chance of Brightie's being in charge won paws down for the Most Terrifying Happening Award of the day.

Kessen spent the last few months sharing all of his stories with me. He even told me that I was ready to take over his position as neighborhood storyteller. This was an awesome responsibility, but Kessen said he had the utmost confidence in my ability to carry on his legacy. With his penchant for honesty, he wouldn't have told me this unless he really believed that I was up to the task. Still, I will greatly miss his guidance and above all, his friendship. We had a rocky start together when I was just a young, impish puppy. But, under his direction, I became a dedicated service dog and returned home to ultimately carry on his skillful art of storytelling. I knew in my heart that I would never be as good as he was at storytelling, but I certainly would give it my best canine effort. The most important thing to Kessen was effort because this counted more than the outcome. In my heart, I knew that he was proud of me, but his trust was the best gift he could ever give to me.

Even though he planned on passing on his position as

pack leader to Brightie, he left me his most cherished possession…his raggedy ring toy. Parting with that toy had to be difficult for him, but that gesture only made his giving it to me even more meaningful. I promised him that no matter how many pups tried to take it from me, I would mightily defend it just as he protected it while he was here with us at the sorority house.

Cherished Gift

The thought of my defending his ring toy made him laugh because I still allowed Brightie to use her femininity to get whatever she wanted. Since I wasn't able to resist Brightie's charms, he wasn't sure how I would ever manage to fend off puppies whose primary weapons were their sharp teeth. I reminded Kessen that if push came to shove, I still had techniques that might handle both adversaries. Brightie was and always would be the epitome of glamour in canine form, and I gave her high marks for that because she lived up to her nicknames of Brightie Girl and Sweet Cheeks on a daily basis. Creating a strobe-like appearance to her face by rapidly blinking her eyes was extremely hypnotic, but I also knew her weakness…she could be bribed. Anything from a small morsel of dinner kibble to a peanut butter-filled rubber bone served as bribery material.

On the other paw, puppies were different adversaries and necessitated a different approach. I'd have to use my wits to outsmart them. The prospect of using my brains to protect his precious toy sent Kessen into a laughing frenzy. While that should have offended me, I recognized that my limitations in the brainpower department might present a problem, but I didn't have to worry about that right now. Brightie wouldn't come close to even touching that toy because of its raggedy appearance, and Harley still thought he'd lose his masculinity if he touched it. I'll admit that I told him the story as a joke when he first arrived at the sorority house, and for whatever reason, it remained a distinct threat to him. Brightie might have her feminine ways, but I had some techniques of my own…no matter how shallow. If they worked to my advantage, I could live with the occasional but useful distortion of facts.

Unfortunately, Kessen left us a short time ago for what he termed his retirement. I'll never forget his advice and how he handled his preparation for going to the Rainbow Bridge. All of us at the sorority house, both canine and human, missed him on a daily basis. Everywhere I turned, I felt the loss of my special friend. I kept his ring toy safe in my kennel and slept on it every night. At times, Dad wanted to wash it, but that might wash away the memories of Kessen playing with it. Because they shared such a strong bond, Dad wasn't ready to do that. I understood how he felt because I even felt a closeness to it in spite of it having a slightly pungent aroma. No matter what condition it was in, that toy was safe in my kennel for now.

Harley was spending the holidays with us. Each time I attempted to lure Harley into mischief, a voice in my head sounding very much like Kessen's, warned me not to even think about it. Hearing this warning, let alone having a voice in my head say it, was enough for me to think twice about getting Harley into trouble. Remembering the rumor about Kessen's spirit lurking on the agility course was enough to keep me on the straight and narrow path of appropriate behavior. Besides, there might be some truth to the existence of spirits, and I wasn't taking any chances.

With each passing day, more and more holiday decorations were put up, and the house gradually took on a festive appearance. Garlands, deep green in color, gracefully draped the fireplace mantle with vibrant red bows marking the placement of our Christmas stockings. Each stocking had our name etched in colorful glitter and by Christmas Eve would hold numerous toys and treats. While our mom tried to space them apart evenly, she ended up leaving a vacant space where Kessen's stocking used to hang. Instead of a red bow marking that area, she positioned a stunning gold bow as a reminder of his absence as well as how much he was missed by everyone. Each time I looked at the mantle and saw the gold bow marking the empty space, a wave of sadness washed over my entire body. Even my hackles lacked their enthusiasm for excitement during these moments. Forcing myself to think of some special times shared with Kessen seemed to bring me back to reality, and the sadness was temporarily gone. Holidays, especially Christmas, were supposed to be filled with joy and laughter. Nevertheless, this holiday season was becoming a real bummer for me.

About two weeks before Christmas, our dad brought out the mini-tree. While its presence with its miniature twinkling lights and metallic ornaments usually signaled the taking of the annual Christmas card photo, the tree didn't spark the same enthusiasm as in past years. The folks usually required us to wear those ridiculous red and white collars having noisy bells hanging from them, but there was no hint of the holiday attire in sight. Even initiating the Tradition of

Turmoil didn't seem quite right under the circumstances. Fooling around by creating chaos while the folks attempted to take a picture of us wasn't really appropriate this year. Harley, being a young puppy, was goofy enough on a good day without guaranteeing more silliness by telling him of the Tradition of Turmoil. Just the thought of having him trying to sit still while wearing a collar with bells was enough encouragement for us to keep our mouths closed regarding our past photo practices. What he didn't know won't hurt him…at least for this year.

Even the folks weren't as enthusiastic as in past years. Mom wasn't scurrying around with her camera, and Dad wasn't selecting special treats to hold our attention during the photo shoot. In fact, they never even took a group shot of us. We found out later that they used individual pictures of us for the annual Christmas card. Apparently, they felt the same sadness as we did during this first Christmas season without Kessen.

We didn't know it at the time, but things were about to change for everyone in the household. Last year, the folks put up this huge tree in preparation for Christmas. Even though it was artificial, it was quite a good imitation of a real tree minus the fragrance. Fond memories surfaced as I remembered our dad's struggle to bring it up from the basement. Kessen, Brightie and I stood cautiously off to the side with our mom as Dad wrestled with this enormous tree in his attempt to get it through the kitchen doorway and into the living room. If the tree had been a real one, we would have believed that he went to a forest to cut it down instead of just bringing it up from the basement. That tree almost touched the ceiling in terms of height and width-wise looked comparable to a satellite dish found on the roof of an apartment building complex. While its girth blocked a bit of the doorway to the sunroom, each of us had to admit that it definitely was a tree worth remembering. Even the fairly tall, artificial Ficus tree, positioned in the other corner of the living room, was dwarfed in comparison to this huge tree.

The folks decorated it with the usual Christmas trimmings…colored ornaments of various shapes, glittered bows and white twinkling lights. As I recalled, a garland made of shiny, metallic material was expertly draped around the tree by our mom, and under the tree was a miniature, ceramic manger scene. Even though it was artificial, the tree with all of its trimmings added a lot to the enjoyment of the holidays. This year was quite different because we all lacked even a glimmer of holiday spirit.

In an attempt to set aside some of the sadness and bring some Christmas cheer to the household, our dad decided to buy a freshly-cut tree. While we didn't know what to expect, he came home a few hours later with a much smaller, yet perfectly shaped, version of the artificial one from last year. Dad proudly announced that this tree, a Fraser Fir, was one of the more popular trees used during the holidays. The tree's needles were dark blue-green in color, and the branches turned upwards just a bit giving the tree a very full appearance. It was certainly different from last year's tree. According to our dad, the tree's marvelous fragrance would last throughout the entire holiday season. We could tell that he was extremely proud of his purchase which was an impressive contribution to the holiday season.

The struggle to get it through the kitchen doorway wasn't nearly as difficult as with last year's monstrous tree.

Carrying this tree was smooth sailing until our dad attempted to put it upright in the stand. It kept falling to one side and then the other. Finally, the tree was secured in its stand and placed on a display table. Dad kept turning the tree until it was positioned correctly in the corner. Mom, looking at it from

Christmas Magic

every angle of the room, supervised his attempts and finally gave her approval of the tree's placement. Our dad, exhausted from his struggle with the tree, sat down on the floor. Seeing him sitting on the floor was just the encouragement we needed to run across the room and jump all over him. It was quite the sight...our dad fending off three, highly excited, jumping dogs. In the middle of all of the commotion, we heard our mom laughing at the spectacle. It was the first time since our Kessen left that laughter was heard in the house. Our dad's getting this fragrant, freshly-cut, Christmas tree brought back the holiday magic, and suddenly, the tree became spectacular in our eyes.

Mom and Dad decorated the tree with twinkling lights, red ornaments of various shapes and gold bows in a variety of sizes. At the very top of the tree and completing the decorations was a petite angel whose hair style must have either survived some sort of explosion or never experienced the use of a hair brush. Her hair, wildly going off in all directions, framed a kind and gentle face. Surprisingly, that wildness in terms of appearance presented an entirely cohesive look when viewed as the vigilant angel atop the special Christmas tree. Somehow, the angel's presence brought back more of the much needed laughter to the household, and in my heart, I felt that we were now just about ready for Christmas.

That night when everyone was asleep, I heard our mom moving around in the living room. Perhaps she was looking at the tree and deciding if our dad had to move it in one direction or the other when he woke up in the morning. I'd have to wait until then to find out. Because the events of the day were so exhausting, I fell asleep as soon as I curled up in my kennel.

Morning came quickly, and Brightie, Harley and I woke up at the same time. We usually had a set routine of running through the bedroom, through the hall, across the living room and out the sunroom door to the dog run. After a while, the folks called us back to the house and served us our breakfasts in the kitchen. This morning, however, our usual routine was suddenly interrupted when the three of us reached the living room. What we saw caused us to awkwardly skid to a stop on the carpet. The sudden action triggered a mass pile-up as Brightie collided with me, and Harley bumped into Brightie. Once we recovered from our collision, we took a closer look at the tree to find out what exactly make it look different from yesterday.

Moving closer to it, we carefully examined the lights and the ornaments but then saw what made this tree extra-special. Silver, paw-print ornaments were hanging from various branches of the tree. Upon closer inspection of the tree, they weren't just ordinary ornaments…they were photos enclosed in silver frames that were shaped like paw prints. We anxiously inspected each shiny frame and discovered that the photos were actually individual pictures of us. That was what Mom was doing during the night when I heard her moving about the living room. With such a heartfelt gesture, she turned the special tree into something extraordinary that reflected our lives here at the sorority house.

Hanging from the branches surrounded by beautiful ornaments and bows were all of our pictures. In addition to my photo, I saw the image of Turin, Brightie, Marnie, Izzy and Harley. Each of us had a position on the tree reflecting the time of our arrival to the sorority household. It was a recreation of the Wall of Fame…only now it was also on our special tree. If only Kessen were here to see this, he'd be so very proud of all of us. With the exception of Turin, Kessen was the leader of the pack throughout each of our lives. He was responsible for shaping our characters as well as our futures, and not having him here with us brought back those troublesome feelings of sadness over missing him.

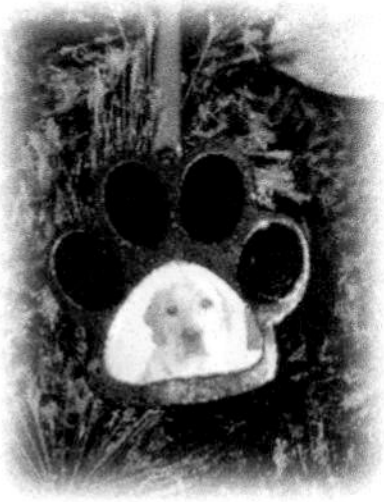

Turin

Brightie

Marnie

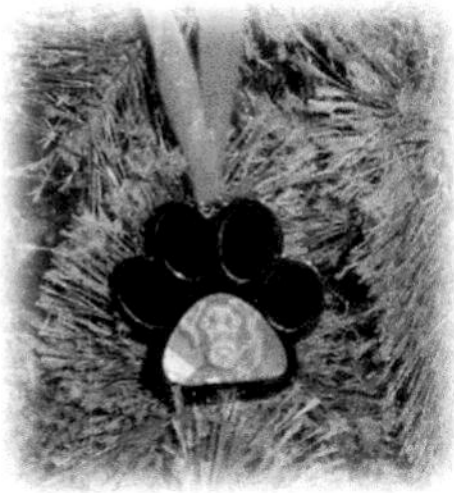

Izzy

Tansy

Harley

Of all dogs to notice this, Harley asked me why Kessen's picture was at the top of the tree while his own picture had a position on a much lower hanging branch. Although I hated to admit it, Brightie and I rarely listened to Harley, but what he was saying this time thoroughly intrigued us. Apparently, in our excitement of trying to find our own individual framed photos, neither of us looked at the very top

Kessen

of the tree. There, directly under the protection of that petite, vigilant angel in a position that reflected his pack order status was a framed photo of Kessen. He was here with us after all...if only from his lofty position on our magical Christmas tree.

Fond memories of all of our experiences together flooded my mind as I stared up at his photo. He had given me another special gift that I'd receive every year when the folks decorated the Christmas tree with those shiny, silver paw-print frames. While I'm not sure that our dad will get a tree quite like this one next year, we had to remember that anything was possible in this household...only time would tell.

Now, passing that decorated fireplace mantle with our Christmas stockings hanging below those vibrant red bows, I didn't feel the sadness anymore about the vacant spot where Kessen's stocking used to hang. Instead, the absence of his stocking reminded me that all I had to do is look up at the tree to see his smiling face. Seeing him there and sharing his stories from the Wall of Fame had a profound healing effect on me...perhaps on all of us who knew him and enjoyed his storytelling.

A few guests arrived later in the day and somehow the conversation turned to Kessen. Our folks and guests laughed as they shared stories about Kessen. Mom talked about how he got his head caught in the fence rails when he was just a tiny puppy, while Dad remembered how proud Kessen was when children read to him as part of the library's reading program. One of the guests believed that one's spirit traveled from one place to another or from person to person as a means of continuing life's journey. She also thought that maybe the same transition occured in animals. That belief sounded pretty confusing to me, but I did remember the rumor about Kessen's spirit haunting the agility course after angering the agility gods. He forfeited his victory in the competition by grabbing the towel from under the seesaw and using it as a victory flag as he ran around the course. While I was not sure about the existence of spirits, I never wanted to take a chance on angering the gods. Brightie, Harley and I listened intently as they shared more stories about the special dog that meant so much to them, but the theory regarding the spirits lingered in my mind.

Brightie, Harley and I shared our own stories with each other as we gnawed on special bones found brightly wrapped under our magical Christmas tree. Because Brightie had a tendency to fall in and out of love almost daily, she remembered how Kessen was always there to mend her broken heart when love was lost or how he helped her regain her courage and overcome her fear of slippery floors. Harley mentioned the stern lecture delivered by Kessen when he first arrived at the sorority house. Having been given the *stink-eye* when he first arrived was enough for Harley to immediately fall in line at the back of the pack. One of Kessen's lectures that included the *stink-eye* was more than enough for him.

Hearing all of these great memories about Kessen and looking at this tree with his photo represented everything that made him great. He was loyal to a fault, fearless, open-minded, funny and strong…all the qualities of a great leader of the pack. No one could ever take Kessen's place…at best, one might only try to follow in his paw prints.

Brightie, as the new leader of the pack, faced a huge challenge. Following a leader such as Kessen was definitely not an easy task. Her first directive was to appoint me as co-captain of the Socialization Squad. If I knew Brightie and her

reliance on her feminine charms, I would be the one doing most of the work while she got the praise. In a few months, Harley would be going on to his advanced training for assistance work, and I believed that he'd do well in that line of work

The New Pack Leader

because he is such a smart, caring and loving dog. Before Harley leaves us, I'll tell him the truth about touching the ring toy and its relationship to his masculinity. He definitely needed to know the truth about this issue, and I was the only one who might be able to set him straight.

As for me, I intended to share Kessen's stories with all of the puppies who crossed the threshold of the sorority house in the years to come. It was important for them to know what a great leader he was and the huge impact he had on all who knew him. Kessen will live on through his stories as I tell them to enthusiastic listeners. Even though I'll probably never be as good as he was in the storytelling department, hopefully I'll get better since there are many more stories to be shared in the near future. He gave me many worthwhile gifts during his lifetime, but entrusting me with the mission of storytelling is by far the greatest and most challenging of all.

Another puppy will be coming to the sorority house in a few weeks. If a male puppy comes to the house, Harley suggested that we change the name of the sorority house to the fraternity house. Brightie, looking at him while blinking those curly eyelashes, just laughed and assured him it would never happen. The resident diva had spoken.

Although this was our first Christmas without Kessen, knowing that he would always be with us in his photos, memories and stories brought laughter to our sorority house once again and would continue to do so in the years to come. Because he was so special to all of us who knew him, his paw prints will remain on our hearts forever. While this particular holiday season began with much sadness, it ended with a sense of new-found happiness.

The holiday season ended with laughter that continued into the new year. Harley spent some of his remaining time with us because his foster family was scheduled to be out of town when he entered advanced training. They asked our folks if they might take him back to the training facility. Our folks were more than happy to do this, and Harley spent his last week with our family. He and the folks did the usual things that were done during the last week…saying good bye to friends and being blessed by their favorite priest. Brightie and I had both been through that experience and knew how exciting and bittersweet it was.

A few days before Harley was to go back to the facility, one of the trainers called and asked the folks if they might assist with a situation. An individual, who was scheduled to get a trained assistance dog, wasn't able to make the trip to get him. The trainer asked if the folks would bring the dog back to the area after they dropped off Harley. The folks were more than happy to help out in this situation and actually looked forward to having an extra set of paws in the backseat of the car on the way home.

On the day Harley was to return to the facility, the entire family piled into the car for the journey. Momentary chaos ensued as Brightie, Harley and I competed for positions in the backseat. Brightie, asserting her right as pack leader, demanded the middle position. Remembering how Kessen instructed us to listen to her, Harley and I acknowledged Brightie's demand and moved to the right and left of the middle area in the backseat of the car. This time, she didn't even have to blink those curly eyelashes to get her way. Because we complied with her directive so easily, there'd be no stopping her with future demands. Without Harley, I'd be the only dog left for her to boss around. That being the case, my indentured servitude was not only inevitable but soon to begin.

This dog is gorgeous!

Once we reached the facility, we said our goodbyes to Harley and wished him well. No tears were shed because he was destined to do great things for someone in need. After the folks took Harley inside the facility, they came out of the building with a beautiful cream-colored dog...the assistance dog who was going to ride back with us. He sat in a confident manner reflecting dignity and determination, yet there was a hint of youthful playfulness in his eyes. When Brightie saw this magnificent looking canine coming towards us, she tossed her head a bit to fluff up her coat and assumed a stately pose in anticipation of meeting him. Seeing that sparkle in her eyes, I reminded her that the dog, no matter how regal in appearance, was a working dog and already promised to someone in need of his services. She just gave me a snooty look and reminded me that as leader of the pack, it was her job to make this traveler feel welcome, and this was exactly what she intended to do. We were definitely in for quite an eventful ride home.

As soon as the folks got to the car with the assistance dog, they had him jump into the backseat with us. We greeted each other and were told by the folks that he was an English Cream Golden Retriever whose name was Charlie. Brightie and I both giggled a bit because our dad's name was Charles, and his friends called him Charlie. What a coincidence that our dad and this gorgeous dog shared the same name. This trip home promised to be fun-filled since we were already chuckling and hadn't even left the parking lot.

As I looked over at Charlie, I was in awe of his slight

Why does he seem so familiar?

but well-toned body, his stately manner and cream-colored coat. While he didn't look like any dog I had ever seen, I actually sensed something very familiar about him…yet, I didn't know what it was. Maybe it was the way he tilted his head or the twinkle in his eyes that caused a brief flicker of recognition. Suddenly, I was hit with a startling realization…he reminded me of Kessen.

Without any hesitation, Charlie positioned himself in the middle of the backseat. Now there was a confident dog.

Much to my surprise, Brightie said nothing to him about being the leader of the pack or her earlier demand to sit in the middle. She just moved to the side and allowed him the prized position. When I questioned her about this, she told me that she was only giving the visitor the courtesy he deserved. This sudden onset of propriety made me wonder what she'd try next to get his attention. She was never going to win the Submissive Female Award…never has and never will. This easy compliance on her part made me wonder what game she was playing now.

As the car reached the main highway, Charlie did something that took my breath away. While our dad was driving, Charlie put his head on our dad's shoulder and nuzzled his neck a bit. Kessen used to do exactly the same thing when traveling in the car. As Charlie did this, our mom stared at him and closely examined his facial features. Even she noticed something familiar about this regal-looking dog. Charlie kept his head on our dad's shoulder, but periodically turned to our mom and briefly touched her cheek with his nose. Kessen did the same thing to our mom when riding in the car. The situation was getting weird…even for me. While Brightie only saw a handsome, stately dog sitting next to her, I experienced such a comfortable feeling sitting beside him. Although he looked nothing like Kessen, I kept seeing flashes of Kessen's behavior in him. Perhaps all dogs shared these similarities to some extent and did the same things when riding in a car. To be honest, I wasn't sure of anything at this point.

As we got closer to our destination, I tried looking out the window as a means of diverting my thoughts, but I kept coming back to Charlie and his Kessen-like behaviors. Then, I remembered the Christmas Day conversation regarding the possibilities of spirits moving on in other people and possibly from animal to animal in order to continue their life's journey. Was it possible that Kessen's spirit was somehow present in this magnificent English Cream Golden Retriever who was now partnered with someone in need of assistance? It just wasn't possible, and I was probably just imagining all of the similarities. Grasping the concept that Brightie was now fully in charge probably caused me to hallucinate things about Kessen in an effort to avoid facing reality. This interpretation made sense to me and had to be the explanation.

We reached our destination, and the folks got out of the car to take Charlie to his new partner. Charlie thanked us for the ride and moved toward the door. As he passed by me in the backseat of the car, once again I felt the same sensation as before...a brief tingle of recognition, but it was gone in the blink of an eye. As the folks walked the length of the driveway leading to the house with Charlie, he unexpectedly stopped and turned to look our way. When he did this, he looked directly at us as if he were smiling...a smile that indicated that all was good with his life. Upon seeing his expression, any sadness I felt about Kessn's loss was somehow gone and replaced with a sense of peaceful

His journey continues.

acceptance...something that I hadn't experienced in months. Then, he turned and confidently resumed his walk to the house between our mom and dad.

As irrational as this sounds, I now choose to believe that it was, indeed, Kessen's spirit present in this marvelous dog named Charlie. No other explanation exists for the similarities in his actions toward the folks, the sparkle in his eyes, the identical tilt of his head as well as the sensation of calmness that surrounded his body. In addition to these things, his name was Charlie...just like our dad's. There were just too many similarities that made sense of it all. By believing that Kessen's spirit was now free and doing what he longed to do all of his life through Charlie, I no longer felt the sadness over losing him that would unexpectedly creep up on me many times during the day.

I never mentioned my belief to Brightie since she would probably be certain that I went off the deep end of the dog kennel. Besides, she was busy lamenting her unrequited love for Charlie. Sweet Cheeks, a.k.a. Brightie, was now renewing

her membership in the Love Lost Club. Because Kessen wasn't here to soothe her broken heart, this appeared to be my next challenge as a subordinate in her twosome referred to as her pack. When she was not around to hear me, I lovingly referred to our pack as Her Majesty's

Her Majesty

Pack. I'd never say that to her face because she'd probably love it and insist on my referring to her as Her Majesty from that point on. After that, she'd probably demand that I'd curtsy when in her presence. Trust me...that was never going to happen.

We are now headed home, and I actually couldn't wait to get there. After spending time with Charlie, the peaceful feelings renewed my enthusiasm and appreciation for my life. A new puppy was coming soon, and as the co-captain of the

Socialization Squad, I was ready and eager to take on the responsibility of his or her socialization...even if it meant doing most of the work. I took great comfort in believing that Kessen wasn't really gone from us. Instead, he lived on in his stories, our memories of him, photos on the Wall of Fame and the paw-print ornaments that served as our yearly, personal Christmas gifts. He left his paw prints on the hearts of everyone who knew him, and while I was probably the only one who believed this, I think his spirit lived on in this majestic dog named Charlie...a dog who just happened to need a ride to his new home at exactly the same time that the folks were able to accommodate him. In my mind, too many coincidences existed for it not to be real. After all, Kessen's spirit was rumored to haunt that agility course because he angered the agility gods during a competition. Maybe he finally made peace with the agility gods and was free to move on with his life. As I had mentioned many times...anything was possible.

I looked forward to sharing Kessen's stories with the new puppy coming to the sorority house. Following in the paw-steps of such a masterful storyteller was quite a monumental challenge, and my hope was that I shared stories as thoughtfully and accurately as they were meant to be told. Kessen once told me that anything worth doing was meant to be done well. Coming

Kessen was very wise.

from my good friend, mentor and leader of the pack, this was such good advice...advice that I was determined to follow throughout my life.

Wherever he might be, I hope that both Kessen and you, the reader, enjoyed my sharing of his stories as much as I enjoyed telling them in my very first storytelling endeavor called Tansy's Tales...

P.S.

Before I forget...I do have something to confess that I never told anyone before. While going to one of the church services during my training, I did something that Kessen attempted, Brightie knew better than to try, and Izzy seriously thought about doing. When our mom took her eyes off me for a moment when leaving the church, I actually gulped some water from the Holy Water Fountain and, surprise of all surprises, didn't get caught. I planned it, did it and was proud of my success. That's my story, and I'm sticking to it!

The Storyteller

My name is Tansy, and as adventures go, I've had quite an interesting life. My journey began as an assistance dog in

training in the magical place called the sorority house. At first, I was a bit of a paw-full, but the residents of the canine pack set the ground rules for me, and I gradually saw the wisdom of their ways.

The resident dogs of the pack were excellent coaches. Kessen, the leader of the pack, was quite the mentor...smart, wise, sensitive and armed with the optical weapon called the *stink-eye* that he only had to use once...that was enough of a deterrent to disregarding the rules. Brightie, the resident diva, was the image of femininity wrapped up in one bundle of blonde mischief. She had stories that, at times, awakened my hackles and curled my well-manicured nails. She became my best friend and confidante through the years.

Having enjoyed a life of adventure, friendship and service to others, I am most fortunate to now share my retirement years with a very special family. As canines go, I am one, very lucky dog!

The Author

Jennifer Rae Trojan, who writes as Jennifer Rae and is pictured with Brightie, Izzy and Nixie, lives in a suburb of Chicago, Illinois with her husband Chuck and her dog named Brightie. Since retirement as high school guidance counselors, Jennifer and Chuck work with various assistance organizations serving as puppy sitters, puppy raisers and volunteers with animal assisted therapy. In addition to these activities, Jennifer gives presentations at libraries, in schools and to community groups regarding the journey of the assistance dog and how it relates to the writing of her books. Chuck and Brightie, representing two of the characters from the books, accompany her to these presentations.

Jennifer and her husband consider being a part of a potential assistance dog's journey a privilege, an adventure and a true labor of love. The entire family is currently involved with raising Nixie, a black Labrador Retriever, for future assistance.

Acknowledgements

Fostering a puppy for possible assistance, training a therapy dog, rescuing a shelter dog or raising a well-behaved pet are not easy tasks. They are joint efforts among owners, families, friends, relatives, trainers and even strangers who lend assistance throughout these endeavors.

While I thank all of those people who have assisted with training and socialization, there are certain individuals who need special recognition for their efforts with Tansy. As a bit of a twist, I've attempted to thank them in a personal way by including their faces with their names.

First and foremost, I must thank my extraordinary husband, **Chuck Trojan**, for his continued support, enthusiasm and assistance while writing this book. Without his enduring love, endless encouragement and countless proof reading, this story would not have been written.

Many thanks to **Pam Osbourne** who not only served as an exceptional consultant in the preparation of the book but was also instrumental in the final printing process including the book's formatting as well as the design of the cover templates. Her many talents and expertise contributed significantly toward the completion of this book. She is also an awesome and patient friend!

Kim Stephenson, of PawPrints Pix Photography, graciously granted permission for use of the cover photos of **Tansy** and Wall of Fame photos. Her skill and expertise are evident in terms of the quality of her images. Her talent, generosity and patience are greatly appreciated.

Kathleen Deist, the Goddess of Grammar and Punctuation, served as one of the proof readers for this book. Her productive insights as well as constructive suggestions proved extremely helpful in the completion of this book. Having her as a consultant was an incredible experience; having her as my friend is the greater gift.

Deborah St. Vincent, the Princess of Punctuation, also served as one of the proofreaders. She not only critiqued the story's content, but also offered numerous suggestions as to possible changes in punctuation and grammar. Her creative insights provided invaluable assistance toward the completion of the story. I truly appreciated her time, efforts and expertise. Her friendship is also a most appreciated gift.

Mary Krystinak, the Countess of Computers, once again demonstrated her computer wizardry by coming to my rescue numerous times regarding the initial set up of the book, formatting, organizing and preparation of bookmarks and book descriptions. I am so very grateful for her computer expertise, her availability for my work and endless patience while working with me. I am especially fortunate to call her my friend.

The trainers at **Narnia Pet Behavior and Training Center** have provided exceptional guidance not just for Tansy but for all of the dogs we've raised. These trainers shared their expertise through instruction, lively demonstrations and individual attention during each of the classes.

Rachel Woodward, Joy Rittierodt and Nivin Wynn

Rachel Woodward, through her calm demeanor, soothed even the most excitable puppy.

Joy Rittierodt always has new and inventive tools for my tool box of training techniques. She is an awesome trainer!

Nivin Wynn, in addition to her humor and laughter, not only gave me an idea for a situation in the book, but also gave me the extraordinary gift of acceptance with her philosophy regarding life and moving forward through loss. Thank you so much.

Father Slawek Ignasik blessed each of the dogs before we took them to their Advanced Training Programs. Knowing the dogs were beginning the next chapter in their lives with a special blessing from him made giving the dogs up a bit easier. **Father Ignasik** had a special love for each of the dogs, and his interaction with them demonstrated his love. We are so very grateful for his blessings.

Jan Jaeger of Charlotte, North Carolina, became a good friend years ago when we both raised siblings for an assistance organization. I thank her for sharing pictures of her dear Kelyn (Kessen's sister) and Charlie, the English Cream Golden Retriever, for events in the book. While we live far apart and don't talk as often as I'd like, we have a very special bond, and that bond is one of friendship across the miles. Bless her heart.

For many years, **Panera Bread** has been a major advocate for assistance dogs in training. Managers like **Vince Palmisano** and **Don Hansen** have welcomed the dogs into their establishment. In doing that, they assisted in the dogs' journeys toward being silent guardians to the disabled. To acknowledge

their efforts, they were recipients of the **Prestigious Paw Award** from **Paws with a Cause**. **Turin, Kessen, Brightie, Marnie, Izzy, Tansy** and now **Nixie** can't thank them enough for their efforts.

Julia Havey was kind enough to share her wonderful dog named **Linus** with our family. Sweet **Linus**, who specialized in the socialization of puppies, spent time with each of our dogs and worked his magic through his Three Step Action Plan. I am most grateful to **Julia** and **Linus** for their assistance.

Special thanks to the **Mahler Family** who gave **Turin** such a wonderful life. His forever family offered him unconditional love, fun, laughter, canine company and special treats. They shared a special bond with **Turin,** and he returned the love on a daily basis.

Fran and **Michael Saltarelli**, **Steven Saltarelli**, **Carolyn**

and **Adam Doebler** not only gave **Izzy** the extraordinary gift of a forever family, but also reunited her with her BFF **Riggins**. **Izzy** not only lives the life of a princess, but she and **Riggins** share a special bond with the newest family member named **Owen**. We are so very grateful for the special life and love given to **Izzy**.

I do wish to thank those individuals who allowed me to use photographs of their dogs in this book:

Jan Jaeger (Kelyn, Charlie), **The Saltarelli Family** (Izzy), **The Doebler Family** (Riggins)**The Mahler Family** (Turin, Coconut, Casper), **Michael Weimer** (Harley), **The Poturica Family** (Sammy), **Julia Havey** (Linus),**Lisa Kruss** (Wall of Fame individual photos of Kessen, Turin, Brightie) and **Stephanie D. Ascencio** (Wall of Fame photos of Izzy).

Special thanks to the **assistance organizations** across the country that provide puppies for fostering and to the **puppy raisers** who share in the puppy's journey. Fostering a puppy for potential service is an experience that lingers in the heart and mind forever.

Finally, I sincerely thank all **assistance dogs and therapy dogs** for the work they do for others. On any given day, most of us can't even imagine how much they do to help others in need. Special treats for all of you!

CPSIA information can be obtained
at www.ICGtesting.com
Printed in the USA
LVOW01s1817021116
510799LV00002B/2/P